PEERS, TENTS and OWLS

Some Solutions

to Problems

of the

Clergy Today

by

James L. Lowery, Jr.

Morehouse-Barlow Co.
New York

(handwritten annotations:) 3/20/95 Presented to St. Martin's Library the General Seminary, NYC in Thanksgiving for the ministry of Dean James Fenhagen

Copyright © 1973 by Morehouse-Barlow Co., Inc.
14 East 41st Street
New York, N. Y. 10017
Library of Congress Catalog Card Number: 73-84090
SBN: 0-8192-1155-9

Printed in the United States of America

Contents

Dedication

This book could not have been written without the inspiration and stimulation of Laile and Josiah Bartlett, Joseph H. Fichter, S.J., Urban T. Holmes, III, and H. Boone Porter. To them go many thanks.

Encouragement in the work of clergy ministry development, out of which this book grew, came especially from David C. Covell, Jr., Ralph Peterson, and George F. Tittman. The late John T. Whiston must be gratefully remembered, too. And general pastoral support in moving in new directions came from my bishop, the Right Reverend Allen Brown of the Episcopal Diocese of Albany, as well as from my good wife, Anita Wu Lowery. To all of them this book is gratefully dedicated.

I cannot pass by the opportunity to thank for their help Mrs. Helen Corrigan, long-suffering typist, and Mr. E. Allen Kelley, my very perceptive editor.

In a larger sense, this book is offered to all pastors in America. I see the great majority of them as the most creative, intelligent, wide-ranging, and multi-talented, sensitive, professional-level men and women around in the world today.

CHAPTER ONE

The Setting

Introduction

This book is very biased, perhaps unconventional, definitely hopeful. It is a statement by an Episcopal priest who has been first a parish pastor in city and country for a decade, and then worked in the general field of ministry development for three years. It attempts to picture, through the eyes of a man who is living on the fringe of the institutional church, where there is no hard and fast line between the sacred and profane, the perils, challenges and marvels of the present world, and the multitude of places in which he sees the Holy Spirit marvelously at work. After some introductory material, we shall be specifically concerned with three problems, and three solutions to them: professional clergy associations, the non-stipendiary ministry, and clergy as consultants to others outside their own parishes. Thus this study is about and for the clergy; but I think its range of view is wider.

The world of the 1970's is an exciting and perilous one; it can be seen as both threatening and hopeful. In the phrase of Alvin Toffler,[1] it is a "future shock" world characterized by acceleration such as to give us change at a rate we cannot cope with, and a world of "transience" confronting us with mobility, diversity, and wastage beyond our ability to adapt. Not only is the population growing exponentially versus the arithmetical growth of food resources, fulfilling the jeremiad of the Rev. Thomas Malthus of two centuries ago, but the amount of knowledge we are confronted with is exploding and the number of choices each person is asked to make is mushrooming. Toffler points to some new strategies for survival in the use of computers to help make choices, and rejoices that the average intelligent person is now given the opportunity to make more choices than before. He also favorably views the emergence of new life styles and structures, such as the ombudsman and the futurist planner. But the outline is clear. We are entering a perilous, challenging period.

Ours is a revolutionary world. The United States finds itself to its surprise less the dominant power than during the Truman era. The number of voting nations in the United Nations has mushroomed, and many of the new countries were born as little as twenty years ago by revolution. We have been through a period of political polarization at home, with great numbers of groups, young and old, from the Students for a Democratic Society to the populist Wallacites preaching a revolution of structure or expectations. Whereas mainline America has before talked only of *reform* (tinkering with the present structure to make it fulfill its progressive goals) and *radicalism* (going to our roots, redefining our goals in line with our basic purpose), we now hear serious talk of *revolution* (throwing out the old and beginning again with new purposes and goals and a totally new vision of society).

In this setting, most of the major institutions of society find themselves under fire; the educational and health care institutions especially are being accused of operating for their own benefit rather than the betterment of society. A certain amount of this comes from a revolution in expectations. The majority of Americans for the first time in history expect to receive a decent secondary and college education. Likewise, the majority now expect access to quality medical care. And both expectations are not being met. Hence the questioning of the institutions charged with forward movement in these areas.

In this context, it would be surprising if religion, one of the major institutions of our society, were not also called into question. A time of rapid social change has brought challenges to the institutional church, and the church is responding with difficulty, because she misses the social props she has been able to rely on for the seventeen hundred years since the Constantinian settlement.

The Post-Christendom Church

Beginning with the Battle of Milvian Bridge in A.D. 313, when the Emperor Constantine embraced the Christian faith and put the cross at the head of his legions, Christianity has been accepted, made official or semi-official, and encouraged by western society. By 1900, the majority of the world's people, under the influence of western colonialism's support of missionary effort, were Christian. What followed from these centuries of church and state working hand in hand, was a culture composed of meanings and values in which Christianity and folk ways were inextricably bound up in one matrix, or as Bishop Stephen Bayne says, "one glorious cultural soup."[2] Bishop Samuel Wylie calls the total situation, which was characteristic of the church's life for almost two millennia, "the establishment church"[3] in contradistinction to the "frontier church" of the apostolic and sub-apostolic eras. This was the "Era of Christendom."

But a vast change has come about in the years since World War I. Whereas 1900 saw the majority of the world's population adherents of the Christian faith, now Christians are less than 30%. The church is again in the minority, even in the United States, according to the latest statistics on church membership. But from her establishment days, she retains certain privileges, such as tax abatements in the U.S.A., and her leadership holding membership in England's House of Lords.

But her position of honor is no longer universally a position of respect and authority. In many ways, the church is looked on as a tired old lady trying to hold onto her considerable worldly goods, buildings, and finery. Some see her as hopelessly divided within herself; others as preoccupied with institutional survival. Still others see her as incestuously concerned with her own inner life. And others see her as irrelevant, ineffective, and expensive. A final group see her as a deterrent to religion, which they must then seek outside her institutional borders. Here the religious revival, especially among the youth of today, is concentrated in an interest in emotions and mysticism, and a kind of mindless fundamentalism typified by many of the "Jesus people." There is a thirst for mystical experience and meditation, so one runs to the swamis; a thirst for community, and so there is experimentation with communal living; and a thirst for self-knowledge typified by the encounter group movement, but much of this deliberately outside institutional religion.

It is my contention that this situation is as much an opportunity as a difficulty. The more the church declines in numbers and honor and status, the more it becomes a minority movement where membership is costly, the more it is a challenge as well as a comfort to belong, the more the remaining church will be free to do her thing in celebration, edification, and mission.

But in this period of rapid change, in this era of switchover from establishment church to post-Christendom frontier church, one group of Christians finds the transition especially difficult. I refer to the ordained clergy, who for centuries have been dependent upon the institutional church for financial support, assured status in the community, and psychic support all around. None of these backings can be counted on any more. Let us take one example: what the sociologists call clergy support systems. They do not support any more.

Supports

Parish pastors look for support above, below, behind, to the left, and to the right. The *above-support* system is the bishop, district superintendent, general presbyter, or judicatory executive. While in many traditions there is the custom of these being the pastor to pastors, today this relationship is failing as a support system. Two typcial studies, in Provinces IV and V (southeast and midwest) of the Episcopal Church, show clergy turning to outside professional help and to outside lay help before their own ecclesiastical superiors.[4] One of the reasons is the increasingly specialized nature of the modern world, which makes an executive of a denomination more and more weighed down with administrative responsibilities, some of which often conflict with his pastoral role. This tendency is accelerated in a period of rapid social change in which the very institutional existence of the church is threatened.

The *below-support* system of the ordained clergyman is the laity in his congregation. The amount of support being given these days is a much more moot question than formerly. On the positive side there is the finding of studies that a pastor often looks to a wise and godly layman successfully for support. Sometimes this person is completely outside the congregation, but sometimes he is in the congregation, and sometimes even a person especially selected or chosen to fulfill this function. But on the other hand, two negative tendencies show up. One of these is the tendency of congregations to look to the pastor for comfort rather than challenge,[5] and not to have much of an idea of him as a person who is also in need of ministering. The other is a tendency of many lay people, frustrated by an increasingly impersonal system in which they find little chance to have their influence count for something, to take out their frustrations on the parish clergy in a situation which is one of the few remaining ones open to personal ventings of feelings.[6]

The *behind-support* system is the one holding strongest. It is the wife and nuclear family of the ordained clergyman. The Province V study alluded to above shows the clergyman first turning to his family for support. A survey of eleven per cent of Episcopal clergy done as a part of a three-phase study by the Strategic Research Services Unit of the denomination's Executive Council in 1969-70,[7] shows the wife of the clergyman as being an almost unfailing support to his professional life. My question about all this, however, is simply to ask if it is not a great deal to require of the nuclear family for it to be the primary support system, counteracting the goldfish bowl aspect of rectory life, and a professional support system at the same time. The literature would indicate that the nuclear family in the 1970's is having a rough enough time under manifold pressures. Even more burden is thrown upon the clerical family. The result is an increasingly large number of marital breakdowns.

Next comes the *left-hand* support system — laymen in other professions. Here the record is good, but sparse. The studies cited above[8] show the clergy turn for help to outside professionals such as psychiatrists, professional marriage counsellors, and casework agencies as a first choice. But the desire is for these to be nearby, and most of them are in distant metropolitan areas, while many clergy are located outside such areas.

Finally comes the *right-hand support* system. Real continuing peer support by other pastors is lacking to clergy, who have on the whole been trained in the lone-ranger academic-researcher model by graduate seminaries. Rectifying this is a primary aim of the growing movement for clergy associations and professional academies, to which subject the most extensive chapter (III) in this book is dedicated.

Different Clergy Reactions

Thus, in a time of rapid change in which all institutions, including the church, are under fire, the clergy find themselves beleaguered without needed support systems. But before going further, it might be well to separate the clergy into three distinguishable groups, whose modes of action vary considerably. I cannot cite statistics or studies, nor can I claim exact reasons for segregating the clergy into thirds. I can only say that this typology comes out of the experience of one who has been a parish pastor in small and large congregations, in city and country, and who finds he is a rare bird in the ethereal research circles in which he moves, in knowing from extensive personal experience the feel of the ordinary church situation.

The top third of all the clergy I see as the cream of the crop — some of the most creative, aggressive, intelligent, sensitive, and wondrous professional and executive people in the world today. They are ten-talent, multi-skilled individuals of tremendous ability. They surface and lead creatively no matter what happens or what obstacle will stand in the way.

They are a self-generating bunch of individuals with many specialist skills, but yet an orientation to the wholeness of being which comes from their vocation and experience. They have been able to deal actively with the situation which challenges them. For them the challenge is really an opportunity.

The second third of the clergy are what I would call the solid middle. They are not great initiators but solid workers, trying to deal with every difficulty as it comes along and to better themselves in order adequately to deal with it. They do not see visions, but they plug away at things and, if outside help is available, can use it and muddle through. For them a difficult time can be handled if help is available.

The bottom third I call the "walking wounded." They are people who came into the ministry with some warmth and talents, but who have left behind their humanity under the pressures and rapid changes. They retreat into a corner. They have become incompetent, ineffective, and the tragedy is that few of them were that way on ordination. They are wounded, beaten and mauled by the fast-changing world. In the days of assured status and place, the world of the establishment church, the world of Christendom, all of these three types of clergy could "hack it." But in the frontier world, the post-Christendom world, only the top third is living triumphantly in adversity, the middle third is coping with the outside helps that are coming on the scene more, and the bottom third, sadly enough, is just not coping.

Problems and Solutions

Among the many problems facing the clergy in this time of turmoil is a leadership vacuum. Perhaps they don't breed them any more like they used to. Perhaps the old Victorian paternalistic style of leadership is no more. Perhaps if leaders larger than life did arise, the world would not accept them as in former days. In any case, there are no great men leading the church forward. This is true from Roman Catholic to Baptist, Episcopal to Lutheran. There has been a vacuum since the days of Martin Luther King and good Pope John XXIII. In this vacuum there has appeared a completely new phenomenon, the clergy association/professional academy movement, with pastors putting their own shoulders to the wheel as a talented group of creative peers.

Another problem is that of too many too-small churches, or many non-viable local ministry units. This may be a relic of an antique hope for a church at every crossroads, or it may be the result of inflation and specialization raising the number of communicants it takes to support one professional pastor. The point is that what now exists is too many small places putting all their resources and effort into maintenance, with no sights raised high. A solution more and more in use in the main line denominations is the part-time non-stipendiary fully-trained "tentmaker" clergyman who frees up salary money and makes the congregation again viable for ministry and mission, as well as maintenance.

A final problem is the over-educated and under-employed clergyman, spending much of his time doing things he need not have two graduate degrees and a good deal of special training for. The appropriate solution in more and more cases can be clergy using their much training and many talents to become accredited in special areas and serving as professional consultants part time to people, congregations, and agencies, and in areas outside their own locality, while bringing in other specialists to their own area.

Thus we have a tale to tell. It is a tale of solutions to problems. It is a tale of "peers," of pastors together in groups and clergy associations; of "tents," worker priests earning their living in secular endeavors corresponding to the tentmaking of St. Paul; and "owls," who are wise consultants helping others beyond their own parishes with their energy and brainpower. I trust it will prove a tale of the Holy Spirit at work in very lively fashion.

Footnotes

1. *Future Shock;* New York, Random House, 1970.
2. Address, Episcopal Diocese of Albany, Annual Convention of 1970, Saratoga Springs, New York. *Cf. Diocesan Journal,* page 71, in which text is *not* given; personal notes used.
3. *Precede the Dawn;* New York, Morehouse-Barlow, 1963.
4. "The Priests of Province IV — A Study on Pastoral Development" done for the Synod of the Province of Sewanee, June, 1971, by Jonn Benton, Helen Benton, Nora Wilson, and A. J. Wilson, III. Available from Episcopal Counseling Center, 240 Plant Av., Tampa, Fla. 33606.
   "Report on Questionnaire on Mental Health and Continuing Education Needs of Episcopal Priests," done for Pastoral Development and Study Committee appointed by the Bishops of Province V, by Paul L. Doerring, Psychological Institutes of Michigan, Birmingham. Available from Bishop John P. Craine, Episcopal Diocese, 1100 West 42nd St., Indianapolis, Ind. 46208.
5. Stark, Charles, Ringer, Benjamin, and Babbie, Earl, *To Comfort and to Challenge,* Berkeley, University of California, 1967.
   Hadden, Jeffrey K., *The Gathering Storm in the Churches,* Garden City, Doubleday, 1969.
6. *Cf.* Bishop John M. Burgess of the Episcopal Diocese of Massachusetts, at a winter meeting of the Massachusetts Clerical Association, Trinity Church, Boston.
7. Series of about a dozen research reports (Level I — data reporting; and Level II — tentative conclusions), "Top Priority Empirical Research Project on the Clergy, 1969-70," Executive Council, Episcopal Church Center, New York (Strategic Research Services Unit).
8. Province V and Strategic Research, *Op. Cit.*

CHAPTER TWO

The New Vacuum

The difference for executives, parish pastors, and lay people in the church between the early 1950's and the 1970's is enormous. It confronts us with a radically new situation.

The Top Leadership

In the 1950's, the higher clergy and their headquarters led the church. There were great men, they led the institutional church into new ways, the church followed them, and in so doing moved forward. The mind is still invigorated and inspired by the mention of such names as Pope John XXIII, Cardinals Richard Cushing (missions), Spellman (Buildings and finances), and Meyer (social responsibility). Dr. Martin Luther King led the way morally, and in my own Episcopal denomination there was the sage and saintly Presiding Bishop, Arthur Lichtenberger.

The point is that the action was where these men were. There was a great deal of experimentation and development to deal with new problems and opportunities, and much of it was associated with or surfaced through the agency of national and international church leadership. Let me take an international case and two examples from my own denomination which seem typical and instructive to me.

Examples of National and International Leading the Way

The man/woman today breathes in a different religious atmosphere due to the labors and findings of the World Council of Churches' long range study of "The Missionary Structure of the Congregation" authorized by its third assembly at New Delhi in 1961. The study was coordinated by the Department of Studies in Evangelism and carried on through regional projects all over the world in the 1960's. Two things about this study are worth bearing in mind as affecting every churchman in every main line Christian congregation. The first is a new mind set about the place of the church in the Christian dynamic. Before, the approach to the church, both as institution and as the Mystical Body of Christ, the People of God, was that the Holy Spirit acted in this fashion: "God-Church-World." The finding of the World Council of Churches study was that in reality most of the time the dynamic action of the Holy Spirit was "God-World-Church" and that often the function of the church was to discover where God was already at work in the world and to join him there. One result was the decision to train missionaries not to go abroad to take Jesus to the heathen, but to live there as fraternal workers seeking to find Jesus "because he is already there" and to relate him to the local scene. A result for the American church was that many actions, such as the civil rights movement, were seen both as a judgment on the institutional church[1] and the channel of much spiritual benefit, in which Christ was present, and from which the church could well learn. An example would be new forms of the traditional religious vows of poverty, chastity and obedience apparent in civil rights workers laboring for subsistence compensation only, not marrying because their work was too demanding and income too small, and communal following of decisions jointly made.

A point to bear in mind was that this turnabout in attitude came about because finances and manpower were present and put to work to draw the lessons and communicate them around the world. The period from the end of World War II to the mid-1960's was, in the United States at least, a period of great institutional growth in membership and buildings and a relatively easy time financially, in which more money both absolutely[2] and proportionately could be "separated" from the local parish and go to the national level, for overseas and national work, and to domestic development, experimentation, and research. It was a day of a fourteen to sixteen million dollar national income in my own three million-member denomination. (The 1970's, by contrast, even with inflation, is a time of ten to eleven million dollar budgets.) Thus money could flow to National Council of Churches and World Council of Churches projects, such as the study of the missionary nature of the congregation mentioned above.

One new thrust the Episcopal Church put much money into in the 1950's was a new and more encompassing approach to Christian education, conceived as a total adult-teacher-child complex, commonly known as the Seabury approach, after the Sunday School curriculum which was a part of it. Similar thrusts came in other communions, including the Roman Catholic Church, which was stunned by the 1948 Italian elections and the successes of the Communists in drawing the Roman Catholic vote.

The Roman Catholics learned that they had not trained their people to distinguish between Christian values of individual freedom, and totalitarian statist values. Similarly, Episcopal chaplains returned from World War II to testify that the men they were charged with preparing for honorable death in battle brought little in the way of Christian knowledge, faith, and values to die for. The indictment they pressed upon the Episcopal Church resulted in a large investment of time, effort, and money in a new approach, involving basic heritage texts plainly written for adults; group life training for parishes; the principle of beginning with adult worship, life, and group training; the tying of classes to parish family worship and community life; and finally a new church school curriculum for ages five to eighteen. Only a minority of parishes used the curriculum materials developed. But the whole denomination was affected positively, thoroughly, and creatively by the process which developed the curriculum. It took much pioneer planning effort and manpower. And the leadership thrust and initiative came from the national church headquarters and structure.

Perhaps the most notable example of leadership into new thrusts forward can be seen in what was called the Joint Urban Project of the Episcopal Church in the 1960's. The key persons in this effort were Bishop Daniel Corrigan, head of the Home Department of the Executive Council under Presiding Bishop Lichtenberger, and the Joint Urban Project Director, George H. J. Woodard. The process put into operation involved all segments of the denomination and included studies of the church in society and a discplined process of data gathering, restructuring, and reporting to the denomination and the ecumenical church, using ten to twelve pilot jurisdictions, at least one of which was markedly rural (Idaho), as a control group to the others. The results were significant. Just as at the end of the 50's the Episcopal Church had a new awareness of and approach to education, so the denomination at the end of the 60's had a new awareness of the societal context of institutional religion and a new comprehension of how planning and development principles could be applied to ecclesiastical programming and thrust in a contemporary culture. Thus for a period of two decades, the national staff and headquarters of this communion, backed by sizable experimental and developmental monies, definitely led its constituency.

The same era also saw, according to theologian Harvey Cox,[3] the emergence of "a new breed of clergy," a considerable group among the clergy of the main line denominations who had switched from a social service way of meeting problems to a political mode of doing so. Another way of saying the same thing is that this group wished to do preventive medicine rather than ambulance driving and emergency room procedures. They were pro-active rather than reactive, seeking to affect the system and avoid ills rather than to bind up the wounds of the victims of the ills. Their religious commitment was and is the same. But their plan for implementing the commitment was different. They stand in a long tradition of the anti-slavery, anti-child labor pastors in days of yore. And they stand in church politics between the pietists, on the one hand, and the "church going Bourbons" on the other. They are organized regionally and nationally into caucuses and pressure groups, along with like-minded laity, either around a whole renewal program for a denomination, as in the Methodist Renewal Caucus, or around a single issue across the ecumenical spectrum, as with Clergy and Laity Concerned (about Vietnam). There are effective networks of caucuses across denominational lines, such as civil rights, black, and chicano groups. Members of these networks in a real sense feel closer to each other within the total Christian community than with many other members of their home communities or denominations. Again leadership came from the national level, and money was available for work at the cutting edge.

Change in the 70's

The advent of the 1970's has seen a drastic change. While the new breed continues to be an active force, its financing is not as solid and its leadership not as united. And within the churches there is real financial trouble and a leadership vacuum.

A look at a week's newspapers suffices to show the split among civil rights organizations. Among blacks, the National Association for the Advancement of Colored People has officially withdrawn from the Black Coordinating Congress attempted in Indiana in 1972. Jesse Jackson and People United in Service to Humanity are separate from the Southern Christian Leadership Council. This list could go on and on.

Financially the main line denominations are suffering. Episcopal national headquarters budgets, as stated before, are now ten to eleven million dollars rather than fourteen to sixteen million dollars, as in the 60's. The United Presbyterian Church in the U.S.A. has suffered a similar setback. The United Church of Christ has had to do away with a whole division of its national organization on social justice. The National Council of Churches budget is down approximately twenty-five per cent. Giving is sufficiently down in the Roman Catholic Church for the National Catholic Bishops' Conference budget to be cut in 1972-73 by three-quarters of a million dollars. And a large amount of church money is having to go to finance debts incurred in palmier days.

Perhaps the most drastic result to be seen publicly has been in two radical reductions in national staff in the Episcopal Church. The first "turkey shoot," as one old war horse of a bureaucrat calls it, reduced professional staffing by twenty per cent in 1969-70. A second cut in 1971 decimated the remainder by fifty per cent.

One result has been a shift in the national effort of the Episcopal headquarters from a leader-experimenter-developed style to a come-on-the-scene-after-the-action, switchboarding -interconnection style. Money goes out to deficit-financed jurisdictions and to already-committed programs. Next to nothing moves forward beyond the survival level, with two or three desperate exceptions, such as community organization and ministry problems. The attempt of the remaining professionals is to coordinate by connecting those around the nation who are doing something significant with those who need information about their successes. This switchboarding style is simply not working out at the national headquarters level, because the time lag is too great and the national headquarters people are too reactive, after-the-fact, not seeking out. In the denomination the picture has changed from national leadership to national muddle. The action is in the many local and special places, parishes, and agencies which are finding a multitude of ways forward. There is active and helpful communication through many *ad hoc* networks set up by these local units, but little in the national headquarters non-network!

Thus the leadership story is of a decreasing national budget, decimation of national staff, and the action not being with highly-placed experimenters who are backed up with encouragement and money. What are the causes of this change? Has there arisen a lesser breed of men in the 1970's? Or is a whole different set of forces at work?

It would be easy to blame the persons presently at the top of the hierarchy. But the matter is not so simple. For the causes come from a change in ethos as much as from the actions of people.

Root Causes

The first cause of the decline of national initiative and the national leadership vacuum is the dynamic and principle of selection of the top leaders, be they bishops, general presbyters, or general secretaries. The methods of selection seem to be a secondary thing, for many of the same dynamics and principles apply to the congregational, presbyterian and episcopal polities. The majority of ecclesiastical leaders in our generation are selected by "cronyism," because they do not make waves, and for past successes in raising money and increasing numbers. None of these criteria are valid in a day of a minority church on the frontier, with decreasing numbers and funds being the norm — in a pre-Constantinian situation. The criteria used apply to an establishment setting in which things go well if one leaves the pre-set machinery alone, and the right thing in that situation is not to rock the boat. The distinguished sociologist Andrew Greeley sees this in the American Roman Catholic episcopate[4] and has applied the term "cronyism" in this setting. But the same could be applied to the Anglican bench of bishops and most of the Methodist and United Church of Christ head divines. We are dealing with a bureaucratic-administrative mind set which reproduces itself in the next generation of hierarchy, like selecting like. But we have crossed the great divide. The way of fulfilling the church's mission in the future is not to select persons who brought in people and raised funds in the days of easy pickings in the past. Something deeper is needed. What we see now results from old principles of selection procuring leaders in a new and different day.

The second cause of the troublesome vacuum is a change

in the type of leadership acceptable and effective today. Until recently the Victorian type of monarchical leadership and decision-making was much in vogue. It lingered on a bit longer in the conservative ecclesiastical institution than in other areas. But the type of approach that accomplishes things acceptably nowadays is participative leadership and decision-making, wherein persons at all levels have a share and their initiative is encouraged. The top leadership's function is to enable, identify, and state consensus, and to be the catalyst for negotiated bargains between differing elements. Such a style can accomplish much, but the crucial foci are lower down. There is less decisive action at the top level. Compared to the former approach, there is a vacuum at the top because the strength and action reside at a middle or lower level.

A third factor causing the leadership vacuum of today is the inappropriate use of a generalist approach in a multiplex world requiring special skills and talents. Many of the clergy have the right talents, but they are not sought out and used. The old saw is still abroad in the land that the clergyman is the only generalist left. This is just wishful thinking, I believe. There is no such animal as "the parish priest." There are those in specialties by situation, such as neighborhood pastor, downtown city priest, town and country priest; and there are those in specialties by function, such as religious education specialist, new-church specialist, community development specialist.[5] Therefore, the need is for the top hierarchy to concentrate on administrative, managerial, and communications skills. But the usual situation, unfortunately, is of leaders so lost in the administrative morass that they are scarcely able to plan, manage, coordinate and communicate. In other words, they are not able to concentrate on leading. This is another cause of the "leadership difficulty."

A fourth cause of the leadership problem in the 1970's is the holdover of a centralist approach in a day of decentralization. Witness the attempt to use common liturgical texts for English-speaking people who "do not share the English language" but who use the same words with very different connotations. Common texts are not necessarily helpful to heralding the Kingdom of God in Roman Catholicism, Anglicanism, and Lutheranism, from Australia to India to Alaska to Junction City to Canterbury. But this is a direction the authorities have moved in, nonetheless, in the International Consultation on English Texts. Roman Catholicism has transferred some authority away from Rome to the National Bishops' Conference, but there are ways in which the national approach to Roman Catholicism may tend to lessen the difference between dioceses which is important for experimentation and renewal. The approach to Christian education is much more centralized in the United Church of Christ in the United States than before. And the classic awesome case, in the age of decentralization, is the recommendation of a commission on function and structure of the Lutheran Church in America, partly acted on in the summer of 1972, to centralize radically the work and authority of the denomination in its national central mission office!

A final cause of the leadership vacuum in the churches, perhaps the one most close to the real base of things, is in a whole new set of lay loyalties — new attitudes in the ninety-nine per cent of the people of God whose missionary call comes through baptism and not subsequent ordination. Perhaps the best commentator on this scene is a man who is both a professional planner and a United Methodist clergyman working with congregational boards across the land.[6] His thesis is that clergy can no longer count on the unquestioning support of the laity in the pew. Says he, "The loyalty button is out of order across the land," and this is as true for the church as other institutions. Lay people expect more of a say in finance, worship, goal setting. Robert Townsend's "Up the Organization"[7] approach — that people work and participate in an organization because they agree with its goals, take satisfaction from its work, and are important parts of its functioning — presumes the kind of leadership that recognizes the layman's talents and gives him opportunity to use them relevantly, turning away from the "big daddy" approach which wants lay people only for paying, praying, ushering, and strawberry festivals.

Results

And what are the results of these forces at work? They seem, to this author, to be a credibility gap and a communications gap.

There is a credibility gap for some. Andrew Greeley's statement about the American Roman Catholic scene[8] is that "Many priests under forty no longer believe a thing the collective hierarchy says, no longer take seriously any of their instruction, and no longer have any confidence in their capacity of lead." I believe this to be a credibility gap, and not just a generation gap, because the same studies by Greeley show the majority of all ages not agreeing with the papal teaching and encyclical on birth control, and because in many places the old and young seem to adjust better to change on the religious scene than the young middle-aged. In the Episcopal Church a regional study on the pastoral development of clergy almost failed completely because the national church headquarters mailing service was used, and the vast number of recipients in the Southeast (Sewanee) Province of the United States simply saw the New York return address and threw the mailing, unopened, in the

wastebasket. Such is the very real credibility gap between
national hierarchy and the pastor on the local scene.

A communications gap also exists. A 1969 study
commissioned by a national Episcopal agency showed that
communication between the church headquarters and the
local clergy was much more difficult to establish than
between the American Medical Association and doctors and
the American Bar Association and lawyers, even in terms of
simply conveying information. This study dealt with
communication from the top down. But we have also seen
the difficulty of communication from the bottom up in a
new world where the action is at the local parish and special
ministry and community level, and the national structure is
simply not effective in picking up information and
switchboarding it to persons who need it.

Your author feels able only to point to the reasons for the
lack of top leadership. He cannot assign priorities to the root
causes; nor can he place the blame. What he can do is
two-fold. First he can urge the church to accept the loss of
old-style top leadership as a basic fact of life for the 1970's.
Second, as a consequence, he urges looking for leadership at
lower levels, such as the local parish or special ministry unit
or the judicatory level. And the chapter to follow is
concerned with the surfacing of just such leadership at that
level.

Footnotes

1. King, Martin Luther, Jr., *Where Do We Go From Here,* Boston, Beacon, 1968,
paperback; *Why We Can't Wait;* New York, New American Library, Signet,
1964.
2. Article on resources past and present; pp. 13-15*ff., Episcopalian* Magazine,
November, 1970.
3. Chapter 3, *On Not Leaving It to the Snake,* New York, Macmillan, 1964,
1965, 1967.

4. Greeley, Andrew M., "Comments to the *Ad Hoc* Committee on the Implementation of the Priesthood Study," Chicago, National Opinion Research Center, 1972. A good text is available in the Feb. 18, 1972 issue of the *National Catholic Reporter* (Documentation Section).
5. *Cf.* article by James D. Glasse, *Christian Ministry Magazine,* January, 1971.
6. Lyle Schaller of the Yokefellow Institute, Richmond, Indiana. The points enumerated here come from an address he delivered as part of the proceedings, 3rd Annual Meeting, Academy of Parish Clergy, held in April, 1962, in Kansas City. Cassette or text probably available from Academy of Parish Clergy, 3100 West Lake Street, Minneapolis, Minn. 55416.
7. MacGregor, D., *The Human Side of Enterprise,* 1960. His "theory" is cited by Robert Townsend in *Up the Organization,* New York, Fawcett World Library, 1971, pp. 119-125.
8. Greeley, *loc. cit.*

CHAPTER THREE

Peers

Introduction

At least partially filling the leadership vacuum apparent at the end of the 1960's is a movement whose watchwords are peer support and pastor's initiative. This movement sees the action as taking place in great part in the church at the level of the local unit of ministry or mission, whether parish or special agency or *ad hoc* multiplex task force. It sees a pregnant force for renewal and evangelism in the skills, talents, and work of the great mass of parish and clerical practitioners. It seeks to enable these men and women to do their thing to the glory of God, the rejuvenation of the church, and the conversion of the world. I refer to the clergy association/professional academy movement of priests and pastors across the ecumenical spectrum.

Clergy associations had their start back in the 1920's, with the founding of the Unitarian Ministers Association. But it was the latter half of the 1960's which saw them coming to the fore, proliferating across the land. Some were and are angry-young-man radical groups. Others are very conservative societies. Some came proudly out of a trade union background, such as the Hawaii Episcopal Clergy Association, which received help from the AFL-CIO Carpenters Union (Jesus *was* a carpenter!) in that state. Others followed professional society routes, such as the Academy of Parish

Clergy, which is modelled on the American Academy of General Practice in the medical world. Two things are evident. The movement is mushrooming, involving, directly or indirectly, 40,000 of the 180,000 pastors in America today. It is part of a general American movement for participatory democracy, though it arises out of a special background of clergy having an amazing array of talents developed in the course of the practice of ministry.

Nature and Definition of a Clergy Association

But what is a professional clergy association? It is an organization of ordained clergy/professional church workers seeking better to equip its members for their mission as effective church leaders by 1) improving working conditions, 2) upgrading the whole professional career process, and 3) providing strong peer support. (Hence the title to this chapter!)

The first area, improving working conditions, denotes the whole field of physical, legal, and economic enablement for mission. This means salary, compensation, and perquisites; due process; standard contracts and letters of agreement; mediation and arbitration of disputes, misunderstandings, and grievances; and the provision of civil and ecclesiastical counsel. In the second area, the intent is to raise standards, skills, and competences; and to raise the amount of participation by *practitioners,* as distinguished from overseers and specialists, in recruitment, selection, training, licensing, accrediting, development, career development, continuing education, objective evaluation, and retirement. In the third area, the attempt is to provide disciplined collaborative peer support and overcome the lone-wolf, knife-in-the-back competitive syndrome. Clergy associations have been and are accomplishing much in these areas.

Clergy associations are professional associations, not trade unions. Associations and unions share the same elements, but they are held together in a different balance. The trade union movement has from its inception (in which clergy and churchmen were significant from the beginning in this country)[1] emphasized the same three elements: 1) working conditions, especially pay; 2) the brotherhood of the working men ("brother" is still a common term used by veteran unionists at chapter meetings); and 3) the upgrading of the work. In the latter respect it is worth noting the landmark agreement reached at the initiative of the steelworkers union with Kaiser Steel over the integration of automation into assembly line production on the West Coast, and the intiative the Airline Pilots Association has taken over the years on airline safety practices, first besting the U. S. Postal System on who would decide as to when weather conditions were safe for flying the mail,[2] and then watch-dogging the Federal Aeronautics Administration on faster installation of proper instrument landing systems at all commercial airports.[3] The action of both professional associations and trade unions involve the same elements. The difference is that in the resulting mix the true professional association puts the emphasis on the upgrading of the professional's service while a trade union puts its emphasis on working conditions and pay. There may be some unions which are very near professional associations (such as the Airline Pilots Association), and there may be some professional associations near to a union, but the difference is there, and the clergy associations, as the reader will see, are definitely professional associations.

Another difference between the two kinds of organizations is that the union ultimately will strike, and the professional association will not do so. Clergy members of associations will never refuse to preside at worship, teach the faith, and do pastoral care.

Three Problem Areas and Three Responses

The reason the clergy association movement is a lively and creative one is that it seems to mushroom into activity in response to real needs and problem areas, three in particular.[4]

The first problem area is that of support systems for clergy. Genevieve Burch, in a significant study of United Church of Christ clergymen,[5] expresses the opinion of a number of scholars in the ministry-studies field that any executive-level worker needs a support system which provides professional support against the vagaries of a hiring organization which might exploit him or her. And the literature of career development counsellors dealing with clergymen[6] shows that clergymen feel not even minimally supported in the financial area, as well as being forced to bear the brunt of a situation which hinders ministry and mission and puts all the pressure on institutional survival alone. The week before putting these words to paper I attended a clergy get-together in the Episcopal Diocese of Massachusetts, at which the bishop reported to his pastors his worry at seeing a rising number of competent, godly men under pressure from their congregations, who seemed to be taking out their frustrations about the changing world and the changing church on their rectors and pastors, and his seeing a need for peer support in this situation.[7]

Clergy associations deal with this lack of support system for clergy by instituting and maintaining various sorts of disciplined peer-support processes. For example, the Iowa Conference Chapter of the Association of United Church Ministers planned to raise a pastors aid fund sufficient to

support a man and his family for a year. The purpose of this
fund was to provide for the man forced out of his cure for
taking a controversial stand on a moral, social, or religious
issue. The fund was to be an instrument to protect him from
financial persecution and to give him a year to find other
work consistent with his career goals. A second example is
the AUCM intent of setting up special dossiers on
"pastor-eating parishes" which have a history of breaking
their clergy leadership, pastor after pastor. Most congregations in the given state conference do not have the resources
and ability to search for new pastors on their own. The plan
is for the conference to refuse to suggest any names to
congregations on the association lift of dossiers until such
time as the congregation is willing to sit down with
consultants from the clergy association who will volunteer
their assistance to help the congregation examine what it is
that seems to be harming the ministers they call, and in this
light to set some goals and prepare a realistic job description
for future pastors.

The second problem is that of working conditions. Some
studies show that, in terms of real money, the compensation
level of Episcopal clergy, for example, has gradually been
sinking over the last forty years. The rewards of status and
honor have themselves become less over recent decades,
witness such popular literature as Vance Packard's *The Status
Seekers.*[8] He describes not only the decline in income, but
also a decline in the prestige which might compensate for it.
It must be added that there is a certain level of income
beneath which the effectiveness of ministry is drastically
hampered because the pastor is so worried about dentist's
bills and food costs that he is unable to concentrate
effectively on his pastoral duties. In my last year as a parish
pastor in the Episcopal Diocese of Albany I ran a small

survey on personal needs of diocesan clergy and found, among other things, that eighty per cent of the parish clergy were eligible for Medicaid.

Clergy associations bring to these problems an array of legal, economic, and physical resources. The January, 1972, newsletter of the Washington Episcopal Clergy Association, one of the most potent organizations in the land, reports that in the last five years, not only has the diocesan mean salary been raised several thousand dollars, but that whereas the total compensation had been far below the government standards for adequate compensation for the Metropolitan Washington area, now the compensation was in excess of the minimum standards.[9] One of the stellar contributions of the National Federation of Priests' Councils to the moral and psychological effectiveness of American Roman Catholic clergy came as a result of its financing the ecclesiastical appeal of the "Washington 44" (subsequently "Washington 19") summarily suspended by Cardinal O'Boyle by the Canon Law Association of America in Rome. (See section on N.F.P.C. below.) The main result of this action has been the creation, in the vast majority of American Roman Catholic dioceses, of arbitration boards on a permanent canonical basis and the consequent establishment of due process machinery at the diocesan level.

The third problem area is the "passive posture of the clergy."[10] The attempt of clergy associations and professional academies is to deal with this by enabling clergy to take an active part in making the decisions for and implementing programs in recruitment, selection, training, licensing, continuing education, setting of standards and ethics, objective evaluation, deployment, career development, and retirement of pastors. A case in point would be the handling of a whole section of the continuing education

effort of the Episcopal Diocese of Oklahoma by the clergy
association of the area, especially in the area of sensitivity
training. Many Oklahoma laymen see this kind of training as
"pinko" and will note no funds for it. The clergy association
arranges such training for interested clergy and lay people.
Leadership is increasingly skillful and sensitive to the group
process as a result, and everyone is helped, including those
who deny the project official support!

The classic case of a clergy association enabling the church
to face her mission in all three areas is ACID (The
Association of Clergy in the Diocese — of Missouri,
Episcopal) around St. Louis. A very few years ago the
minimum stipend in the diocese was $4,700, plus housing.
And there were fifteen clergymen in the diocese whose
stipends were below the stated minimum. The action of
ACID, then enrolling approximately one-third of the clergy,
was as follows. Member clergy took a regular day off each
week. On this day they obtained the most public secular job
possible, for instance, clerking in a hardware store on Main
Street. The cash earned by the entire group of clergy on their
"days off" at the end of a year was paid out to the clergy on
substandard support, bringing them up to the stated but
not-met minimum. This action was done publicly enough for
the diocesan convention at its next meeting to be shamed
into meeting its own standards. And at the following annual
meeting, the bishop (who had been trying unsuccessfully for
increases along these lines for some years and who was
secretly "in cahoots" with ACID) was able to raise the
diocesan minimum (in just twelve months, mind you) from
$4,700 to $6,700.

When the stipend was thus raised, ten missions (aided
congregations without full autonomy, some of which had
been on the dole for a good century) faced for the first time

in decades a solid threat to their very existence. The increased financial requirements might put them out of business. Some of the missions began to ask for the first time such basic questions as "How can we stay alive?" "What is a church really supposed to be doing in Smithville?" What other ways of ministering are options in Jonestown?" And for the first time in their history these congregations considered the basic questions of Christian mission, all because of a push for a salary raise by a clergy association. The clergy effort involved peer support of deprived brethren, bettering of working conditions, and the rethinking of effectiveness for mission, and this is what a clergy association exists for.

Unitarian-Universalist Ministers Association (1920's)

We have presented the clergy associations/professional academies as a growing movement dealing with a leadership vacuum in the church. We have seen something of the nature of such associations and the kind of problems they deal with, as abstracted from the life and actions of many of the associations. Now we turn to a selected description of national groups in the clergy association movement — their history, their concerns, and their victories for their cause. We begin with the great-granddaddy of the movement.

The oldest denominational clergy association is the Unitarian-Universalist Ministers Association, founded in the 1920's as the Unitarian Ministers Union. In 1961, subsequent to the merger of the two parent denominations, it merged with the Universalist Ministers Association to form the U.U.M.A. at an organizing meeting in Swampscott, Massachusetts.

Over 650 of the over 880 "Uni-Uni" ministers belong. It is a denominationally recognized and encouraged organization and holds it annual meeting in conjunction with the annual gathering of the denomination. It receives office space at 25 Beacon Street, Boston (the denominational headquarters) where it pays for the services of one full-time and one half-time worker, who keep the membership list, handle dues, maintain records on the group life and major medical insurance programs, and process claims. Annual dues are fifty dollars.

This first clergy association has involved itself significantly in insurance matters. Unitarian pastors found themselves covered by a denominationally administered, endowed pension plan that came through with a grand total of $1,600 per year upon retirement after a lifetime of service. In the 1950's the clergy association sparked a contributory insurance plan for amounts above the set minimum and in the 1960's a health plan. The U.U.M.A. now administers an enlarged group life arrangement and a major medical plan.

Much of the nature of U.U.M.A. must be seen in the context of congregational polity, which is treasured by Uni-Uni people. Each congregation is the sole determinant of its own affairs, including the relationship with its minister. The minister-congregation relationship is seen as unique. Any national affiliation is regarded as strictly voluntary and only for fellowship, communications, and larger services to be rendered. It follows that Unitarian-Universalist ministers feel similarly about any national organization, including their own clergy association. Thus one might buy insurance, health, and professional services from many places, one option being the Ministers Association. The Unitarian-Universalist Association and the U.U.M.A. lay down suggested guidelines, not mandatory rules, and sanctions for enforcement are few and far between. Be that as it may, any organization with seventy-five per cent of the pastors in the denomination does have considerable influence. Hence the title of the Bible of the U.U.M.A.: "Guidelines."

The guidelines cover salary minimums and stipends, remuneration for professional services, housing, fringe benefits, conference costs and professional expenses, leave, specific working conditions; candidating, contract, and severance; institution and departure; job description; non-parish, supportive, part time, and emeritus ministry; former ministers; with appendices covering continuing education, two specimen sabbatical plans, a code of professional ethics, and a feedback sheet to the organization to be filled out by users about experience with the guidelines. It is a comprehensive compendium, with its constituent parts periodically updated.

Of special interest are the two kinds of sabbatical suggestions: one for metropolitan areas, and the other for ministers in isolated or rural situations. Suggested fee schedules for remuneration for professional services (such as one per cent of established minister's salary plus twelve cents per mile for a Sunday's supply work) and specific remuneration levels for participation, theme talks, leadership, etc. of a conference are interesting. Also the statement that long tenure in a congregation is helpful *provided* the minister and congregation grow together, and it is in this context that sabbatical leave is considered.

The functions of the U.U.M.A. are defined in its constitution and bylaws as "1) to assist ministers and churches in interpreting the ministerial function; 2) to improve the professional capabilities of Uni-Uni ministers; 3) to cooperate in relationship with the Unitarian-Universalist Association and other denominational agencies and institutions in recruiting, training, maintaining and strengthening professional standards and the prosecution of mission, clarification and promotion of the message of religion, provision of security for the ministry, establishment of adequate salary standards; 4) to promote and protect the professional rights and status of its members in relationship to churches, agencies, one another and the general public; 5) to define the principle of freedom in all churches and denominational relationships; 6) to formulate a code of professional practice and to provide for the support of this code with a censure of violations."

So far as this author knows, the U.U.M.A. "code of professional practice" is the only document now in existence in a clergy association which covers the waterfront. (The United Church of Christ does have a suggested official denominational statement, but it is not as detailed or all-encompassing.) At this point, pressing interests of the U.U.M.A. are: the establishment of a grievance committee, involving a "good offices" man of the U.U.M.A. residing in each geographical district of the denomination; advocating pastors having a say in the criteria for and the distribution of ministerial welfare funds; and making the "code of professional practice" effective over the whole clergy of the denomination.

Association of Episcopal Clergy (1966)
National Network of Episcopal Clergy Associations (1971)

Once upon a time there was a unique character, mind, and bishop named James Albert Pike. He pursued four careers: the law (including arguing before the Supreme Court); the Pentagon (Navy and governmental bureaucracy); the church; and, at the end, a weird mixture of theological apologetics, research into Christian origins, and spiritualism. Some say he asked all the right questions and gave all the wrong answers. Some say his heart was in the right place but that he was such a reductionist that he threw out the baby with the bath water. Some say that he was one of the most marvelous apologists for Jesus Christ and one of the best pastors the world has ever known. No two people really agreed on him. But two things are accepted by all. First he was a genius, and second he attracted to the San Francisco Bay area during his bishopric in the Episcopal Diocese of California (1958-66) an incredible array of talented people, many of more individualistic, erratic, and abrasive bent than in the normal run of Anglican jurisdictions. They did yeoman work, pioneering work, and much of the reason was that Jim Pike was a superlative pastor to them, always ready with firm backing in the many ensuing controversial situations. It is no mark of discredit to Pike's more main line successor to say that in the subsequent administration persons who have gotten themselves out on limbs for the love of God and man have found themselves more isolated and not given the same kind of backing as by the previous bishop. Anyone who succeeded Pike would have had a difficult time, for James A. Pike's way of operating was *sui generis.*

Suffice it to say that a number of very talented clergy found themselves exposed, on the firing line, being manhandled, and not receiving what they considered to be adequate backing from the persons and institutions they served. The founding of the Association of Episcopal Clergy was, among other things, an attempt to apply the healing balm of due process to these wounded warriors and to save useful persons for further church ministry. (Some are continuing effective service. Some are presently institutionalized. And some have busted out, to do such things as become the most successful insurance salesman and broker ever seen on the West Coast.) Note here how much the emergence of an issue causing great pain had to do with the formation of a clergy association.

The founding president of the Association of Episcopal Clergy was the Rev. Lester Kinsolving, now a nationally syndicated religion columnist, and one on whom greatly divided opinions are held. Around him, beginning in 1964, when he was a mission vicar in Salinas, California, with the encouragement of the bishop, gathered the nucleus of what was to become the A.E.C. Chartered as a national association in 1966, it circularized the entire clergy of the Episcopal Church. By 1967 at the Seattle General Convention of the Episcopal Church, the membership had grown to around two hundred, about half of them within a day's journey of San Francisco.

Just before Seattle, George F. Tittman of Berkeley, California, replaced Kinsolving as president in a move to communicate better with the Anglican establishment, as well as to incorporate the knowledge and influence of persons who had been connected with the unofficial but distinguished Overseas Mission Society of the Episcopal Church. (Note here the intertwining of clergy association and missionary interests.) At Seattle, A.E.C. members led a coalition of groups which for the first time turned the direction of the Church Pension Fund from acting first, last, and always for the benefit of its actuaries, towards acting more for the benefit of its beneficiaries. From this time on, the association also dealt with about four cases of due process each year, and usually ended up, through mediation, with an agreement which, while not wholly satisfactory to either party, was something both could live with. Thus there was for the first time a mediation-conciliation process which could minister to many differences before they exploded into harmful messes with each side taking hard stands. Just as the case of the Church Pension Fund made a national name for the A.E.C. in the national church field, so mediation of a claim by

Executive Director John Morris of the Episcopal Society for Cultural and Racial Unity (a civil rights group which played an important role in pre-Selma and Selma days) against the diocese in which he resided for an illegal refusal to accept his letters dismissory (letter of transfer to a new diocese) made the name of the A.E.C. in mediation and due process efforts. These two cases provided proof of what pastors could do if they joined together in a disciplined, hardworking, and just manner.

It must be added that much of the Church Pension Fund victory was due to a tremendous amount of research and political organization engineered by the A.E.C. group in California, and by the Rev. Canon Richard Byfield of San Francisco in particular. And much of the success of the mediation work came from the carefully organized procedures spelled out in detail in the A.E.C. bylaws and from the use of lawyer-priests on investigation committees.

In the course of its seven years of life, the Association of Episcopal Clergy founded six local chapters: California (San Francisco area); San Joaquin (Central California); Northern California; Texas (Houston): Oregon; and Hawaii. In 1968, it decided to employ two part time field representatives: the Rev. Edward Berey for the west, and the Rev. James Lowery for the multitude of single memberships scattered throughout the east. Both were tentmaker priests, Berey combining his work with the Office of Economic Opportunity and insurance labors, and Lowery with professional and executive level career development consultancy for a Chicago-based national network. Revised goals were set, through the incorporation of a disciplined planning process into the life of the organization. These included 1) to serve as an organizer of local chapters, catalyst to other clergy groups and stimulator of a federation of such groups across the denominational and ecumenical spectrum; 2) to move towards national mediation and appellate systems for aggrieved clergy; 3) to publish and work towards the use of standard contracts between clergy and their employers; 4) to press for regular sabbatical leaves, transferability of theological degrees, and dual accreditation for theological graduates; 5) to encourage the management of pension funds for the benefit of their beneficiaries, and the investment of fund portfolios for the benefit of society; 6) to do research in the area of parochial and non-parochial ministries, stipendiary and non-stipendiary ministries, and to collate and broadcast the results; 7) to organize clergy credit unions.

The years 1969 through 1971 saw the emergence of fewer new A.E.C. chapters but more independent diocesan clergy associations all over the country, from Los Angeles to New York to Washington. The level of local commitment in the independents often exceeded that of some of the A.E.C. chapters. Many of the independents plugged into the Association of Episcopal Clergy communications net but did not wish to be linked with the A.E.C., due to its angry-young-man reputation of some years before, as well as personality conflicts with some of its former leadership. Sensing this situation, the A.E.C. board made a policy decision to allow its representatives either to work on founding new chapters or to act as catalyst/consultants in founding new independent local associations. They knew this might threaten the survival of the national organization, but they also felt their major commitment was to getting the basic renewal job done. We shall see below the results of this decision.

In the period 1969 through 1971, which ended with roughly 250 A.E.C. members and a like number in independent associations (out of 9,000 active Episcopal clergy in the nation) many victories were won on the local level as well as on the national.

Prior to the foundation of the Oregon chapter of the A.E.C., for example, the four diocesan clergy delegates to national church conventions were invariably the rectors of the four largest parishes in the jurisdiction. This meant that these men had quick entry into the episcopal study, while most of the clergy had a long wait to obtain access to their chief pastor. After several years of clergy association activity, three out of four of the national convention delegates are truly representative of the run of the diocese. Only one is of the old "cardinal rector" type. Furthermore, all clergy of the diocese now have rapid entry into the bishop's office. Another result of Oregon association activity is a credit union for the clergy, which is negotiating to work as a revised ecumenical entity with other denominations to form an ecumenical agency in the Pacific Northwest, using as the incorporative nucleus a going program of the United Methodists in the area.

Among the independents, the classic work of ACID (Association of Clergy in the Diocese — of Missouri) has already been described. But we must add that its annual dues of seventy-five dollars are the highest anywhere in the movement. PRIDE in Pennsylvania (Philadelphia) has provided a model in raising ministerial salaries to a level allowing real self-respect on the part of all diocesan clergy, and in watchdogging diocesan authorities to see that diocesan staff fired in the financial crunch were given adequate separation pay. The Long Island group is the only association requesting and receiving official diocesan status akin to that of a senate in the Roman Catholic structure. The Delaware Episcopal Clergy Association was the only one with 100 per cent clerical membership.

The activities of the Washington Episcopal Clergy Association are of sufficient interest and important to rate separate mention. This is perhaps the most conservative and certainly the most potent of any local chapter or association of approximately thirty groups extant in the U.S. Episcopal Church at the beginning of 1973.

The beginnings of W.E.C.A. were in a frustrated "clericus," or infrequent meeting, of the clergy of the Episcopal Diocese of Washington (D.C. and several suburban Maryland counties), which was manifestly an unsatisfactory group and organization to all involved and looking on. In order to deal with the organization as well as to consider the needs of the clergy, two planning conferences were held, involving the clergy of the diocese, the two bishops, and the director of clergy development, a man working half time for the Maryland Diocese and half time for the Washington one. (His employment showed a real commitment to do something in the area of ministry-concerns on the part of the two dioceses and two sets of bishops involved, and this should be borne in mind.)

The result of these conferences was to brainstorm the whole clergy career spectrum, from recruitment through retirement, and to divide it into a number of areas. It was agreed that the bishop and his clergy development man would be responsible for initiative in half of these, with the clergy group responsible for watchdogging the implementation. Initiative for the other half of the areas was assigned to the clergy group, with the bishop and his assistant functioning as watchdogs. At this point, the clergy set up the Washington Episcopal Clergy Association in the Process of Formation, with dues of over fifty dollars, and hired a retired "cardinal rector" of the diocese, the Rev. Dr. E. Felix Kloman, as Executive Director for the salary he was allowed under the Church Pension Fund and Social Security. Kloman has given a good thirty hours a week to W.E.C.A. and clergy association activity ever since. The development process resulting in the formation of the Washington Episcopal Clergy Association on October 6, 1969, took a full year, with the first half devoted to the brainstorming and the second half to the development of the structure. In the end, seventy-seven clergy joined at fifty dollars a head.

Several things should be noted here. First is the "form follows function" nature of this group, which began with need-areas, goals, and only then organized to implement them. The second is the thoroughly American setup of checks and balances, with diocese in certain functions, with review by clergy, and clergy assignments with review by diocese. (It must be admitted that this situation was helped immeasurably by a certain hardnosed trust amongst the members of this remarkably compact and prosperous urban diocese.) The third is the use of a respected clergyman of the diocese, with local and national influence, as the executive director. It is perhaps because of a combination of these factors that W.E.C.A. has been the bellwether local group in the Anglican Clergy Association movement.

Accomplishments of the Washington Episcopal Clergy Association are many. Among them are playing a definite role, along with the bishop and the latter's assistant for parish development, in consultation with parishes regarding vacancies and in assisting with the drawing up and implementation of a placement (deployment) plan; the monthly publication of a list of parish vacancies in five to seven dioceses in the east, which has made possible and respectable the revolutionary practice of clergy directly applying for cures to vacant parishes; representation on diocesan clergy compensation committees; and the passage in convention of guidelines for compensation in five to seven year cycles.

Two documents, produced after much research, have been of great benefit to the whole church. The first is a "model letter of agreement between vestries (or bishops) and clergy." This contractual agreement covers all areas from stipend to continuing education allowance, from study leaves to hours of work expected, from baptismal offerings to mediation of later disagreements of interpretation. The second is a "statement on professional responsibilities and standards." In some respects it is similar to guidelines put out by the Department of Ministry of the United Church of Christ and by the Unitarian-Universalist Ministers Association, but it is unique in being directed only to the clergy, and in making it very clear that it is the responsibility of the *clergyman* to have a contract, or at least a letter of agreement with his church board; that further it is his responsibility not to accept any agreement paying less than the minimum set diocesan standards; and that his fellow pastors will hold him directly accountable if he fails in either of these respects.

One final thing must be added about the style of W.E.C.A. Paid up members only can vote, but plenary meetings and board meetings are open to all clergy of the diocese. And any clergyman and parish may call on the association for services. This avoids cliquishness and secretiveness.

At the Houston General Convention in October, 1970, after preparation done by the eastern field representative of the Association of Episcopal Clergy, two meetings were held with representatives of about sixteen of the then known eighteen or nineteen clergy association units. A tentative move was made toward the eventual formation of a loose network of locally autonomous clergy associations; involving all possible groups, and the Rev. Edward R. Sims, then president of W.E.C.A., agreed to serve as chairman. In May, 1971, in St. Louis, the National Network of Episcopal Clergy Association was born at a meeting attended by local associations and a delegation from the A.E.C. The principles of local autonomy and decentralization were set forth, a program (that of the A.E.C., essentially) was accepted, and each local association received the assignment of implementation in a specific area. The Rev. Mr. Sims was elected chairman to do national administration and to work with new emerging clergy groups. The Rev. Roy Strasburger of Saratoga, California, was elected vice-chairman, and the Rev. Claudius Miller of St. Louis was designated communicator. Each member local association pays fifty dollars a year to N.N.E.C.A., and anyone wishing the occasional N.N.E.C.A. newsletters sends a small subscription fee to the communicator. (A May, 1972, national conference voted to continue this decentralized method of operation.)

The month following, in June, 1971, the Association of Episcopal Clergy voted to go out of business, to recommend that its local chapters join N.N.E.C.A., and to turn over its membership lists to the N.N.E.C.A. chairman. By the end of the year, the organization had been disincorporated in California, its financial affairs settled, and its records prepared for deposit with the historiographer of the Episcopal Church in Austin, Texas, for a permanent record of the first clergy association in the denomination and the second one in the country. Three things are worth noting about this action.

The first is that the Association of Episcopal Clergy felt it was worth going one step backwards in order to move two steps forward. The highly decentralized style contemplated by N.N.E.C.A. would mean the fifteen per cent of the activity which was national and the not-yet-unfolding ecumenical thrust would be very lightly dealt with. Something would be lost in the new arrangement. But at the same time a larger, more broadly-based network would result, with more active local commitment. And this commitment would mean a job better done in the long run.

The second thing is that the A.E.C. was willing to die for a greater cause. Most institutions wish to survive first and then to do a job. This pioneering organization had been willing to threaten its own position by serving both its own network and also putting money into serving as catalyst/consultant to other emerging clergy associations. Then it allowed itself to be swallowed up by a total grouping of seventeen independent and six of its own chapters (having aided many of the independents in getting off the ground). At present there are twenty-four or twenty-five known clergy association groups in the Episcopal Church, seventeen of which are paid up members of N.N.E.C.A.

The third thing is the openness of the A.E.C. In the same manner as the Washington Episcopal Clergy Association, meetings, services, and board conclaves were open to all the clergy. The A.E.C. strategy and debates have always been fully communicated to the clergy concerned and to the church press. At the time of its demise, the A.E.C. was very open about its intentions, its hopes, and its misgivings. This openness has been threatening to some groups and persons who do not know how to deal positively with such honesty in ecclesiastical situations too often honeycombed with secret competitiveness, hostility, and a desire for the surival of the *status quo.* This openness seems to be a basic characteristic of the clergy association movement. With it the movement has done marvelous things. Without it the movement deserves to fail.

A final look at the clergy associaton movement in the

Episcopal Church shows it unique in the respect that the majority of efforts have come out of the local scene in response to local needs rather than out of a national frustration, as with the Lutheran Church in America, or out of the biddings of Vatican II, as with the Roman Catholics. Another unique feature of the Episcopal situation has been a reversal of the usual organizational pattern, from centralized organization to decentralized network.

Some things may be seen here which have been characteristic of the whole clergy association/professional academy movement. First is the use of the planning process in the formation of associations and the provision for ongoing definition of the ultimate visions, goals, implementation, and review. Second is the employment of process facilitators in meetings and developments, and the use of outside consultants in particular settings. Third is the willingness to investigate, to risk, and to fail, as a part of the renewal process of tooling up clergy for mission.

National Federation of Priests Councils (1967)

Under the influence of Pope John XXIII, the bishops and fathers of Vatican Council II (1962-65) enunciated two principles which represented a significant change in direction for the Roman Catholic Church.[11] The principle of *subsidiarity,* encouraging the making of decisions and carrying them out at the lowest (most local and front line) level possible, represented a radical change from the hierarchical principle of from-the-top-down.

The accompanying principle of *collegiality,* or participative peer collaboration in actively carrying out the mission of Christ in church and world, represented a vast change from the monarchical imperialism associated with the Roman Catholic Church for a millennium. Such changes in direction are not easily accomplished. But many instrumentalities have sprung up in the post-Vatican atmosphere of openness to assist in the implementation of these principles. One of them is the priests' councils movement throughout the world, taking initiative in furthering the apostolate at the priestly level. In cooperation with sisters' caucuses, conferences of religious, lay associates, *etc.,* they seem to enflesh subsidiarity and collegiality.

A word about terminology is necessary at this point. The general term for a priests' group is "council" in the U.S. Roman Catholic context. The specific kinds of councils are two: first, "associations," which have no official standing in their diocese and, second, "senates," which either have official standing and sanction or have some of the membership or officers officially appointed.

In the area of priests' councils in the United States, the first activity was the gathering in 1966 of a group in the Archdiocese of Chicago, the largest and one of the weathiest in the nation. There followed the official formation of the Association of Chicago Priests in October, 1966. This organization seems to have been the leader in the formation of priests' associations and senates, as well as in the later organization of the National Federation of Priests Councils. Its high point of membership was 1,250 out of a possible 2,700 clergy in the archdiocese, reached under the chairmanship of the Rev. Jack Egan, a remarkable man who began his Chicago career as Archdiocesan Director of the Cana and Pre-Cana Conference, became the archdiocesan urban affairs man, helped found the National Urban Training Center for Christian Mission and the Regional Interreligious Council for Urban Affairs, was removed from his post by a new cardinal archbishop as part of a concerted withdrawal from an urban thrust, and was given a parish which ran itself well enough for the good Irishman to surface as chairman of the Association of Chicago Priests! Egan now heads the Secretariat for the Catholic Committee on Urban Ministry at Notre Dame and is a founder of the Interfaith Council on Urban Ministry.[12]

The Association of Chicago Priests, presently boasting but 500 members (due to the formation of an official senate in Chicago with the cooperation of the association), is famous for its stimulation of priestly and lay voice in the nomination of bishops, advocacy of social programs, plumping for parish councils, experience in co-pastorates, personal assignment and evaluation board work, and its censure of Cardinal Cody in 1971 for not representing the opinions of the clergy and laity of his diocese at the April meeting of the National Council of Catholic Bishops preparing for the October bishops' synod in Rome on the priesthood and world justice.

As the proliferation of local councils continued, a national structure became necessary for many reasons. In May of 1967, an initial meeting in this direction was held in Chicago, with eighty-five priests present from thirty-five dioceses. The National Federation of Priests Councils was official born in May, 1968, in DesPlaines, Illinois, as a federation of local councils, comprising the memberships of the senates of ninety-three dioceses and the associations of twenty-one dioceses.[13] Father Patrick O'Malley of Chicago served as the first president for two years. By the time of the 1969 annual meeting in New Orleans, there were 130 member councils from 114 dioceses, representing 38,000 priests out of the approximately 60,000 in America. San Diego, 1970, saw Father Frank Bonnike of DeKalb in the Rockford, Illinois, diocese elected president. Baltimore, 1971, counted N.F.P.C. membership at sixty per cent of the 59,000 priests in 122 of the 148 dioceses.[14] At this writing some councils have dropped out (St. Augustine's council was dissolved by the bishop!) but have been more than replaced by new member groups, and Father Reid Mayo of Burlington, Vermont, is president.

The member councils of N.E.P.C. cover a wide spectrum. The only clear-cut distinction is that the senates are official and the associations unofficial. In some, all senators are appointed by the diocesan bishop. Other schemes exist where some are elected by the secular priests, some partly elected by secular priests and partly by religious serving in the diocese, and some are partly appointed and partly elected. Then the actual nature of the council may be different than its structure or composition suggests. For example, according to an anonymous commentator, in the beginning the Boston Priest Senate was given much more power by the inimitable Richard Cardinal Cushing than it knew how to deal with! On the other hand, the council in the Diocese of St. Augustine, Florida, mentioned above, tried a little local initiative and was closed down by ecclesiastical fiat.

In about eight dioceses, there are both senates and associations. In Chicago some fear that the covert purpose of a senate will be to "bust" the Association of Chicago Priests; yet the A.C.P. wants a senate in existence in addition to itself!

The national federation was operating in 1971 on a $175,000 budget. Affiliating councils pay an initiation fee of $100 to $400, depending on their membership size, and then an annual per capita assessment determined by dividing the budget by the total number of priests represented, *i.e.,* five dollars each for the 35,000 priests in member councils. In some cases the diocese pays the council's assessment to N.F.P.C. In other cases it comes out of the council's budget from annual dues. In still others there is a matching agreement. A final possibility is that dues are paid by individual parishes and institutions.

The federation employs five full time professional level persons — the president, communications man, peace and justice man, office manager and administrative assistant — but the brunt of the work is done in committees. These include communications, finance, human resources and development, personnel, priests councils and the laity, research and development, and role of the priest. In addition, interim policy and direction are the responsibility of an executive committee with wide geographical representation, covering the twenty-seven provincial areas in the U.S. There is an effective planning, goal-setting, implementation, and evaluation process built into the life of the organization. Also, "Any national thrust for a program is usually an outgrowth of the initiative of one of the (national) committees. These national committees have fostered a spirit of independence and yet of collaboration. Both are necessary."[1 5]

A word about the seven purposes and the many achievements of the N.F.P.C. may give an additional impression of its flavor. The first purpose is "to promote priestly brotherhood by facilitating communication among priests councils." This is accomplished by regional and national meetings, committees and task forces drawn from all areas of the country, and by the publication of a newsletter, which became a magazine, *Forum,* and ultimately the monthly newspaper, *Priests — U.S.A.,* which goes by subscription to 8,000 of the 30,000 members.

The second purpose of N.F.P.C. is "to provide a forum for the discussion of pastoral matters." The meetings and intercommunication further an exchange of ways of doing things, a diversity in unity which is consonant with the post-Vatican life and style of the people of God.

The third reason for being in the federation is "to enable priests' councils to speak with a common representative voice." Here is a way for the hierarchy to hear the opinions of the front line employees, arrived at representatively. A result is the emergence of many fine leaders from the priesthood whose light would otherwise have been hidden under a bushel. One of the difficulties of being high up is to find ways to make use of the contributions of real talent at the local church level. The N.F.P.C. offers a way for such talent to surface, be heard, and be used creatively.

Fourth, N.F.P.C. exists "to promote and collaborate in programs of pastoral research and action." It has put over $25,000 into the Koval survey of the clergy[16] and several thousands more into a Gallup poll of lay attitudes on celibacy in the priesthood, which made almost as much contribution, in their own way, to research on the problems of the priesthood for the bishops' synod in October, 1971, in Rome, as did the official American bishops' half-million dollar study of the historical, theological, sociological, and psychological aspects of the priesthood.

The fifth purpose is "to implement norms for the renewal of priestly life." One of these was the recognized use of due process, and the case in point was that of the "Washington 19." The importance of the victory won and the field in which gains were made deserve special attention.

In 1968, after the issuance of the encyclical *Humanae Vitae,* some sixty Washington priests said they would respect the consciences of those Catholics who came to conclusions different from those of the encyclical.[17] Over forty of these received summary penalties from Patrick Cardinal O'Boyle. (More than twenty of the original sixty have since left the active ministry.) In the spring of 1969 N.F.P.C. pledged itself to help these priests get a fair and impartial hearing in the church's judicial system. The issue at stake was not the reaction to the encyclical but simple due process. With the help of a voluntary Committee of Concerned Canon Lawyers (members of the Canon Law Society of America), nineteen priests initiated their case through the ecclesiastical courts. They were referred to Washington and Cleveland tribunals. A formal request was delivered to the Vatican Secretariat of State, asking for a judicial review of the case.

At this point N.F.P.C. set April 20, 1969, as a deadline for action if no response had been received. An emergency meeting of the house of delegates of the federation was slated to determine the nature of that action. On April 18 word was received by Father Joseph Byron, petitioner on behalf of the "Washington 19," that a fair and impartial hearing would be forthcoming.

What followed was a three-part judicial review process in Rome in 1970 presided over by Cardinal Wright of the Sacred Congregation of the Clergy. The "Washington 19" were represented by their ecclesiastical counsel under the aegis of the Canon Law Society of America. And 1971 saw the resolution of the situation in mutually acceptable terms, with the suspended priests not asked to recant any statements, and restored to their faculties by the archbishop.

This commentator sees four things especially significant about the case. The first is that without localized set procedures, the case dragged on enough so that at least twenty capable men have been lost to the priesthood. The second is that the N.F.P.C. was on the spot to pay over $15,000 in costs for the proceedings in the ecclesiastical courts of jurisdiction and appeal. The third is that N.F.P.C. was active in pushing the whole matter, but emphasizing the issue of due process, on which communication and dialogue was possible. Fourth (and most important), as a result of the

"Washington 19" case, most American Roman Catholic dioceses now have due process procedures and hearing-commissions. This represents a real step toward a renewed style of dealing with the ministry.

The sixth purpose of the national federation is "to provide the means for priests' councils, united nationally, to cooperate with laity, religious, bishops and with others in addressing the needs of our church in the modern world." Only at the national level can such matters be dealt with adequately. But N.F.P.C. can bring grass roots level concerns to the surface. One of the great contributions made to help American bishops prepare for the October, 1971, Rome synod was informing them that peace and justice were primary matters and the problems of the priesthood secondary in the minds of the great number of clergy.

The seventh and final purpose is "to do whatever is necessary to carry out these purposes." Actions have ranged from a series of symposia on the prayer life of priests to an *amicus curiae* brief on behalf of a selective conscientious objector whose case was before the Supreme Court, relying heavily on the U.S. bishops pastoral letter of 1968, to liaison meetings of the N.F.P.C. executive committee with a like committee of the National Conference of Catholic Bishops.

This observer would make four final comments about the National Federation of Priests Councils. First, it seems bigger than it really is. The membership of the councils is 30,000 plus. But many of the individual men are not active in official senates, whose membership is mostly conterminous with the entire priestly population of the diocese. Second, while there is a wide spectrum of opinion represented in the member councils and individual membership, the N.F.P.C. is less a middle-of-the-road organization and more of a reflector of a plurality within unity. Third, N.F.P.C. has emerged as a strong new force with real influence for innovation and brotherly support. And lastly, of all the national groups it has best succeeded in putting matters of mission and service first and relegating its own concerns to second place.

Academy of Parish Clergy (1968)

The Academy of Parish Clergy is unique in the clergy association movement in having been interdenominational and interfaith from the very start. It also has insisted throughout on its identity as a professional academy concentrating on systematic professional development as a basic requirement for membership. The key word to denote its style is "collegiality," and this term applies both to the brethren within the ordained ministry and to relationships with key professional laymen in the parish and community structure.

The genesis of the A.P.C. is found not in the clergy but in the practice of medicine. About twenty-five years ago, many general practitioners across the nation found themselves threatened with losing their hospital privileges. The reason was not jealousy between specialists and generalists, but the fact that a great many general practitioners simply were not undertaking programs of systematic professional development sufficient to keep themselves informed on health care and medical treatment advances. Hospital staffs were becoming more and more worried about care given and surgery performed by inadequately informed doctors adversely affecting the hospitals' reputations.

The result was the formation of the American Academy of General Practice, membership in which required 150 hours of systematic professional education in each three-year period. Not only has the work of this professional academy restored, in great part, the general practitioner to respectability, but it

has changed the nature of general practice to that of a patient —
and a family-oriented specialty of its own, with its own
standards and skills, and affected medical education in a very
creative way. In addition, the A.A.G.P. is the bellwether
medical organization in requiring regular professional
continuing education in order for a doctor to remain
accredited by professional peers. Seeing this process in
action, the Rev. Dr. Granger Westberg, Dean of the Institute
of Religion, Texas Medical Center in Houston, conceived the
idea of a similar academy of general practitioners in ministry
to play a similar role in upgrading competency and setting
skill standards for pastors in the fast-changing world of the
1960's, in which most seminaries were preparing men better
in the academic aspect of religion than in the actual practice
of ministry. Westberg was convinced that the approach of a
professional academy similar to the A.A.G.P. was a viable
one, based upon studies showing measurable changes in the
skills and competency of ministers in such a process done in
Kokomo, Indiana, and LaGrange, Illinois. (This impression
was strengthened by his later experience in a "teaching
parish" in Hamline, Ohio, in which he worked while teaching
pastoral theology at the Hanna School of Theology at
Wittenberg College, Ohio.)

Westberg published a landmark article calling for such a
pastors' academy in the *Christian Century* magazine in 1965,
before his move from Houston. There began to be a small but
growing network of persons interested in implementing the
idea. What was needed was some seed money, a national
organization, and some solid backing for the idea.

In 1968, Dr. James D. Glasse, then professor at Vanderbilt
Divinity School, Nashville,[18] published his book, *Profession:
Minister,*[19] enumerating criteria for the professional man,
showing their application to the minister as a professional,

and indicating that the unfilled gap was the lack of a professional organization or society for peer support and standard setting. His book attracted attention among the scholarly and the ecclesiastically well-placed. In the same year, foundation seed money enabled this growing network of persons to meet together in Houston and bring into being the Academy of Parish Clergy, Inc. The Lilly Endowment of Indianapolis made a grant to this ecumenical organization to enable it to get off the ground. A three-year grant from the Bush Foundation established a communications network, and further grants from the Lilly Endowment continued support while the Academy moved towards self-sufficiency.

In 1969 its office opened at 3100 West Lake Street, Minnneapolis, with Dr. Henry B. Adams, formerly with San Francisco Theological Seminary in San Anselmo, California, as executive director. Since then the A.P.C. has been busily at work. April, 1971, saw a growing committed membership of over 600 persons (out of a potential of 180,000 parish pastors of all denominations and the 250,000 total clergy of the nation), a $60,000 annual budget, three-quarters of which came from various foundations and one-quarter from memberships and charges, and a great many things accomplished, which could set the stage for more to come. The membership covers forty-four states and five other countries and is increasing its organization on the local level.

The academy is represented on two committees of the American Association of Theological Schools. One of these is preparing new standards and procedures for accreditation. This is the first time in history that parish clergy have had a voice in standards of education by which men are prepared for their own ranks. The other committee is studying ways to measure readiness for ministry before ordination.

The Academy of Parish Clergy publishes a quarterly

four-page newsletter for internal communications and began in April, 1971, to published a journal to highlight case histories of creative explorations of ministry by local pastors.

At its 1971 meeting, the A.P.C. passed a "statement on competency," defining the areas of competence needed in the practice of ministry. It also endorsed the necessity of other ways of theological education as alternative to the graduate resident seminary in preparing for the actual practice of ministry, and it became a sponsor of Inter-Met, an innovative approach to such preparation in Washington, D.C. Inter-Met employs the clinical method, the action-reflection mode, and the theological resources of the Washington area graduate theological schools, under the direction of Dr. John Fletcher.

But the real character of A.P.C. is seen in its method of professional continuing education and in its colleague groups. The heart of its work is the requirement of 150 hours of systematic professional development during each three years of membership, half of which may be in institutions or schools or outside the parish, and half of which is to be systematic study of and reflection upon something in the local parish and community which presents an opportunity for development of ministry, normally using the case study method. The A.P.C. headquarters gives general supervision to this effort and plugs in local parish pastors to area resource people, as well as integrating the individual into local colleague groups. In this respect, the A.P.C. has recently published two of an ongoing series of directories of study projects under way and completed, collated by geographical area and subject matter. The point of the whole procedure is to encourage supervised learning, with the pastors reporting their activity to supervisors and receiving helpful feedback and evaluation. The result is a growing network of local-area groups, which help the members in personal and professional growth, which give real peer support, and which upgrade the ministry — the very marks of a professional association.

One important achievement of the Academy of Parish Clergy is the placing of representatives of parish pastors for the first time in the position of helping make decisions affecting their own preparations for ministry on the international accreditative level. The hallmark of A.P.C. seems to be its stress on collegial interpollination. And not only is this true of persons within the ordained ministry; emphasis is also placed on the colleague group of professionals, the total professional group within a parish or in a community. This is understandable, given the medical association which served as the model in founding the academy. It also leads to the possible use of talented lay ministries so often overlooked by pastors.

A final word about money. A.P.C. is notable, in the whole clergy association/professional academy movement, in its ability to attract funds from foundations sufficient to mount a major program. The lesson may be that foundations give willingly when the membership base is broadly ecumenical and the aims of the group not overly controversial.

Association of United Church Ministers (1969)

The genesis of the Association of United Church Ministers was a summer conference group of forty-five United Church of Christ clergy at the La Foret camp near Colorado Springs in July, 1969. These founding members were from twenty-two states. Since then the A.U.C.M. has grown to around one hundred members, with organized chapters in Colorado, Iowa, Minnesota, Wisconsin and Massachusetts. Membership is open to ministers and other professional employees of the denomination whether ordained or not.

Activity subsequent to its foundation has been largely in state regional groupings. National structure and dues have never been set up officially. Coordinator for the effort from 1969 to 1971 was the Rev. Frank Burr of Humboldt, Iowa, and since 1971 the Rev. Robert Zinn of Waukegan, Illinois. The name of the organization has been changed from the La Foret Pastors Union to the Association of United Church Ministers.

The purposes of the organization are threefold: 1) to bring each individual United Church of Christ congregation or institution to a full and honest facing of its responsibility to its minister (including adequate material support and guarantee of due process in the professional relationship); 2) in the denomination, to give parish ministers a more effective voice in determining policies of the denomination which affect their careers; 3) with peers, to maintain and improve the professional capabilities of ministers through continuing education opportunities.

Following from these purposes are nine specific goals: 1) to assure an adequate guaranteed annual income for all ministers of the UCC; 2) to assure that the treatment of ministers by the churches and agencies is fair and that the ministers and their families are protected from abuse by individual members or by power blocks in the parishes; 3) to assist ministers in conflict with their churches or in conflict with groups within them and to assist ministers with personal problems; 4) to keep a dossier on each church as to the history of its relationships with its ministers; 5) to maintain and improve professional standards and the educational base for minstry; 6) to maintain close relationships with seminaries to be certain that the interests of ministers are adequately served and that each student is prepared for a secular as well as a church vocation; 7) to assist ministers who choose to leave church vocations; 8) to provide task forces to deal with churches on behalf of ministers in crisis or in negotiation; 9) to establish standards which churches should meet in relationships with their ministers.

The A.U.C.M. is an organization which has not yet moved towards its potential, due to a lack of organization and coordination. It is the biased but fervent feeling of this reporter that five out of every six renewal attempts since World War II have failed due to lack of administrative undergirding, lack of communication to the individuals on the front line who either provide the finances or do the work, or because the hierarchy has pulled the rug out from under them when they see that meaningful change is in the making.

In the case of the A.U.C.M., too much of the administration was left to one coordinator who had busy parish responsibilities. No effective national structure ever eventuated. In the matter of communications, excellent reports were circulated, but these were few and far between. In the case of the hierarchy, there was too much reliance on the official teat for money and structural help. Denominational bureaucrats can encourage a passive stance and then, under pressure of other matters, do nothing.

The Association of United Church Ministers pioneered in some exciting new directions, but the organization is not healthy and may well be defunct before the end of 1973.

Ministers Council, American Baptist Convention (1970)

The Ministers Council, American Baptist Convention was originally formed in the mid-1930's "to promote fellowship among ministers of the American Baptist Convention." It sought to provide occasions where ministers could meet to discuss common problems. Early concerns included deepening the spiritual life, counselling, adequate salaries, and placement. A house organ was published five times a year. Over the years, concern with issues such as salaries and placement led to a change in emphasis. But the decision openly to change into a "professional support system" was made only in its 1970 meeting, duly heralded in the religious press. That year was devoted to thinkiing through and making the decision to change the style and nature of the organization. The year 1971 was devoted to communicating the change to the whole membership and potential constituency. Now 1972 is expected to be the year that will tell the tale, in terms of the number of memberships renewed or newly garnered.

The new direction of the council coincided with the presidency of the Rev. Clyde Wolf, pastor of the First Baptist Church of Brockton, Mass. Wolf, a former board member of the Academy of Parish Clergy, seeks to apply the same approaches learned ecumenically to his home denomination. The Rev. Charles Fosberg continues as Executive Director of the council.

Two things must be said about the American Baptist Convention. The first is, in the words of a Baptist preacher who works as a State Council of Churches executive, "Wherever there are four Baptist preachers, there are five different opinions!" Hence a markedly independent way of doing things; and hence also in American Baptistry the presence of both the Ministers Council and the separate Union of American Baptist Clergy, Inc., of which we shall hear more later. Second, the A.B.C. is a denomination which, while it fiercely treasures congregational independence, at the same time has a powerful, centralized series of denominational boards. Paul Harrison, well known sociologist, in a study of the denomination,[20] makes the point that the national denominational boards, headquartered mostly in

Valley Forge, Pennsylvania, wield a good deal of centralized power and take some strong initiatives.

It follows that a semi-official pastors' fellowship organization in the process of becoming a clergy association, having as members 3,500 of the 5,000 A.B.C. parish pastors and 6,000 ordained ministers, has been able to exert quite some push. There are three areas in which substantial successes have been counted: career centers in various regions in the late 1960's, a national computerized personnel support service in the early 1970's, and work during the whole period in the Department of Ministry, National Council of Chruches, and its subsidiary Career Development Council.

The Ministers Council aided in the drive for a series of studies by various denominational groups in the 1960's. One showed a growing number of exits from the parish ministry in the 1960's compared with a generation before.[21] The study showed that whereas twenty years before those leaving generally moved into the ministry of other denominations or into teaching and social work, the more recent drop-outs turned, in roughly equal numbers, to 1) teaching, 2) social service, 3) community development and government, and 4) business and industry. Few departed to the ministry of other denominations. In other words, there was a more drastic exodus to other than the helping professions. Other studies showed the need for continuing education in the theological, communications and behavioral sciences and the need for help in pastoral deployment as well as salary supplementation. A result of these studies (with the Minister Council A.B.C. one of the chief advocates) has been the establishment and funding of a quartet of career centers of the American Baptist Convention, that in Wellesley, Massachusetts, being the pilot one.

The original attempt was to offer helping programs in the

areas of career assessment, placement consultancy, continuing education counselling, and salary support. With the
experience gained at the pilot unit in Massachusetts, other
centers have emphasized career assessment and counselling as
the dominant element of the cluster. A second change has
been at the A.B.C. center in Oakland, California, which serves
as the nucleus for an eventual interdenomination-
ly-sponsored career counselling center on the model of the
Northeast Career Center in Princeton, New Jersey, which
under Dr. Thomas Brown was transformed from an agency
operated by the United Presbyterian Church in the U.S.A.
into a interchurch unit. (Wellesley is expected soon to do the
same.)

Having seen these career centers in operation, I can testify
to their rapidly increasing professionalism and competency.
And their inception in the A.B.C. system was due in large
measure to the initiative of the Ministers Council A.B.C.

A second area of effective action has been that of
computerized personnel support services. The Ministers
Council came on the scene in the mid-1960's, when a
Rockefeller Brothers Fund study for a Church Manpower
System was undertaken by Information Services, Inc., of
New York City. This was done through the National Council
of Churches under the tentative sponsorship of several
denominations, which then lost interest. The A.B.C., through
the work of the Ministers Council, persisted in advocating the
study. In the end, the council recruited the minimum number
of required church bodies (A.B.C., Episcopalians, Lutheran
Church in America, and Department of Ministry of the
National Council of Churches) for the Rockefeller Brothers
Fund to pay for all the technical work by Information
Services, Inc., in setting up four parallel computerized
personnel data listing services, which are proving a great help

in getting hard data to church bodies in the process of choosing pastors, and being an equal help to individual pastors in giving them a national screen on which their talents and skills may be projected. (Subsequently, a fifth body, the American Lutheran Church, has joined.)

The final area in which the influence of the Ministers Council A.B.C. could be felt is the leadership given by American Baptists on task forces of the Department of Ministry, National Council of Churches. Charles Fosberg is on the executive committee of the department.

This commentator finds himself of two minds about this organization. On the one hand, the Ministers Council has done some effective work and is seeking to become a full professional support system. Whether it will succeed in this endeavor is yet to be seen, but it certainly has already accomplished much for the betterment of pastors.

On the other hand, can the Ministers Council be a genuine *peer* support group when the backing for the executive director comes, not from membership fees but from the official Ministers and Missionaries Benefit Board of the A.B.C.? Also, according to the constitution, membership in the Ministers Council automatically ceases when "a member engages in permanent full time secular employment." This rule is a holdover from a previous age and not conducive to aiding the movement for tentmaking or non-stipendiary pastors, which is a concern of men in other denominational associations today. Perhaps this provision will be changed when the restructuring is completed.

Union of American Baptist Clergy, Inc. (1970)

Two or three months before the Ministers Council American Baptist Convention decided to change to a "professional support system," the Union of American

Baptist Clergy, Inc. was founded during the annual convention of American Baptistry in Cincinnati. At the end of two years it had only about one hundred members, but they seem to be located in key places (a large church in a college community in Ohio, the public relations staff of Colgate Rochester Divinity School, *etc.)* and to have a real gift for publicity releases which make their name and needs known.

Membership is now open to any person ordained or commissioned, and to other professionals within the American Baptist Convention, and to any American Baptist student enrolled in a seminary.

According to its constitution, the purposes of the union are 1) to support the development of relationships within the American Baptist Convention which will enable clergy and laity to fulfill mutual ministry and to strengthen the church as an instrument of Christian discipline; 2) to provide an organization which can initiate as well as respond effectively to policy decisions in local, state and national convention situations; 3) to provide supportive fellowship to its members and their families; 4) to mediate controversies and alienations between members and churches, members and convention executives, members and the community; 5) to stimulate efforts of convention agencies in defining and implementing mission to each other and to the world; 6) to understand better the task of clergy and church; 7) to develop evaluation files on churches served by members and help members find positions commensurate with their interests and abilities; 8) to establish and negotiate realistic salary scales for members and an appropriate concept of an adequate field; 9) to provide contractual outlines; 10) to provide effective means of communication to members by members about issues confronting American Baptists at all levels.

The chief concerns of the Union of American Baptist Clergy seem to be 1) the influence of state and national *convention executives* in a denomination with a *congregational polity;* and 2) the possible use of executive power to manipulate rather than to enable local pastors to have satisfying, fulfilling, and effective ministries. The chosen area for action has been the American Baptist personnel services nationally, and with the state or regional convention executives as they are a part of the ministry information network.

The U.A.B.C. supports central personnel information files, individual dossiers, and third party evaluation for use by congregations to help them in calling effective pastors. But its goal is to have the personnel system serve the professional employees as a group as well as the churches seeking pastors. It notes that the Advisory Committee for the Personnel Placement System, which has over twenty members, includes only four pastors, three women, and two blacks, the rest being executive/area ministers. The resulting balance of power and interest is out of line with the constituency the system should be serving and inconsistent with a convention whose polity is congregational. Finally, it sees the domination by church executives as giving great power to a few persons, recognizing the corrupting tendency of unchecked power. It is particularly alarmed by the "unethical practices of some executive/area ministers giving oral evaluations which they then refuse to put into writing, and withholding specific dossiers requested by pulpit or personnel selection committees, creating situations in which data supplied to congregations is not as true, objective and complete as it ought to be." In addition, it feels that dossiers should be distributed to other agents than just executive/area ministers.

I see room for both the Union of American Baptist Clergy and the Ministers Council A.B.C. within the American Baptist Convention. I further see different emphases in the style of the two organizations: the U.A.B.C. pushing for a return of the A.B.C. to its stated polity, emphasizing local decision-making, and the Ministers Council seeking renewal through the structures that exist. Together, in collaboration, they could be quite a force for reform and renewal, as well as serving as checks and balances to keep each other effective and honest.

A subsidiary but important field of activity has been "good offices" or mediation work by U.A.B.C. The controversy that has made their name in this area centers around a Denver parish building purchased from the American Lutheran Church by a black Baptist congregation with a white pastor, where there is some dispute over ownership of the building, method of payment, and the theological and social issues involved. An eviction suit has been instituted, and the Union of American Baptist Clergy is mediating with the two parties.

There is an amazingly high level of ability in this small association. It bears watching far out of proportion to its numbers.

Association of Lutheran Clergy and Professional Layworkers (1970)

The beginning of the Association of Lutheran Clergy and Professional Layworkers was at a meeting in August, 1969, which included Ralph Peterson, former Director of the Department of Ministry, National Council of Churches, recently returned to the parish pastorate in New York City; Hans Goebel, a Lutheran Church of America pastor in Baltimore; and Leigh Jordahl, a professor at Lutheran

Theological Seminary, Gettysburg, on sabbatical at the Ecumenical Institute, St. John's Abbey, Collegeville, Minnesota. These men proposed a renewal and reform movement within the L.C.A. and called a meeting of about eighteen persons in November in Washington, D.C., with a resource person from the Association of Episcopal Clergy sitting in on the proceedings. At this point their worry was simply that their denomination had not sufficiently faced either the contemporary crisis of church and Christianity, or a mandate for continuing reform in the light of the crisis. An American Lutheran Church pastor also sat in and shared his thoughts as well as a document of the A.L.C. on the tentmaking ministry. A representative of the Seminarians Cadre, which had successfully boycotted the L.C.A. psychological examinations for ordination, also explained the influence obtained by his group and how it had defined the issue over which the effort was made. Thomas Myers of York, Pennsylvania, served as the secretary-coordinator of the growing movement.

Another meeting of a still larger group numerically and geographically in January, 1970, defined the target membership as the total pastorate and full time layworkers in the denomination, and the main issue to be dealt with as the hierarchical, paternalistic, and secretive mode of operation of the Board of American Missions, Lutheran Church in America. The various issues in which specific approaches might be made were seen as a not-yet-released report of a ministry board, the use of ecclesiastical economic power, and the deployment of personnel. A theological undergirding for a reform party within the denomination was produced as a working paper by Dr. Jordahl.

The result of these meetings was the founding on May 1, 1970, in Washington of the Association of Lutheran Clergy and Professional Layworkers, with a tentative set of bylaws, a national organization, and at least a dozen synodical (regional) caucuses. Pastor Leopold Bernard of Buffalo was named president and Pastor Myers secretary. The only stand taken at the founding meeting was that the report of the L.C.A. commission on the study of the doctrine of ministry should be openly distributed and discussed, that all pastors and congregations should have a say in producing any recommendation in this area for the L.C.A., and that the newly founded association was opposed to any definite position being taken on the doctrine of the ministry until full hearings should have been held throughout the denomination.

Between the founding convention in May and the first annual convention in October in Cleveland, the following occurred:

1. The A.L.C.P.L.'s request for copies of the report of the commission on the study of the doctrine of the ministry, L.C.A., was refused by the chairman of the commission "because copies were not available . . .for financial reasons, among others."

2. Task forces prepared papers for workshops at the convention in the areas of a) Ecclesiology; b) Church and World; c) Communion and Confirmation; d) Manpower; e) Compensation; f) Role of Layworker vs. Clergy; g) Function and Structure; h) Consortium Ecclesiology.

3. Recruitment literature was distributed across the country, identifying as the purposes for the association:

    a. To promote reform in the Lutheran Church in

America in order to enable the church to fulfill
its mission to the world.

b. To promote professional competence by:

1. Maintaining and elevating professional competence through supporting programs of
continuing education, career development,
assessment, and regularized sabbatical leaves.

2. Identifying and sharing common needs and
responsibilities, both personal and professional.

3. Working for the establishment of an effective
placement system within the L.C.A.

4. Aiding in the development of more functional and relevant patterns of theological
education.

5. Disclosing and working for the alleviation
and correction of injustices which may arise
in relations between church boards or
congregations and synodical presidents and
other clergy or professional layworkers.

6. Seeking just levels of compensation.

The October, 1970, convention elected an enlarged central
(steering) committee and a new secretary, Marilyn Miller of
Liverpool, New York. The first official notice of the
A.L.C.P.L. was the attendance of George Hoog, Director of
the Personnel Information Center, L.C.A., who served as a
resource person to the manpower workshop. By this time, an
association member was sitting on an advisory committee to
Pastor Hoog's personnel support services groups. (It is worth
noting here that Episcopal, L.C.A. and American Baptist
Convention clergy associations have all succeeded in having
members watchdog their denominational computerized

personnel information listing services, in determining the kind of information that would be fed into them and sent out to persons using data, and in general being helpful in setting up such services.)

Between the first annual convention in 1970 and the second national convention in February, 1972, considerable progress was made. First, membership increased to over 220 pastors (three per cent of the denominational clergy). Membership growth seemed to be restricted to pastors only, however.

Second, actions of synodical caucuses on local and regional issues were seen as justifiably taking up a major part of the association's efforts.

Third, a regular newsletter began to appear, put out by a publicity committee headed by chairman Richard Dowhower of Pittsburgh. Fourth, the A.L.C.P.L. saw the need to join in an ecumenical clergy association network, having used outside resource persons from seminarians and other clergy associations at the very beginning of its life.

Most important, due to the A.L.C.P.L. effort, the Lutheran Church in America publicized its report on the study of the doctrine of ministry and subsequently held open hearings for its revision at the request of the national denominational convention. The association was one of the groups testifying at the hearings and the only critical group appearing from outside the denominational establishment.

It appeared that the report recommended a sweeping redistribution of power in the L.C.A. in the direction of centralization, away from the parish and synod to the national structure, just at the time the need for decentralization was being recognized in the secular world. The stand of the A.L.C.P.L. was twofold: first, that centralization would lead to rigidity in prosecuting the mission of Christ; and second, that there should be increased participation of the whole L.C.A. constituency in making decisions.

The major concern of the February, 1972, national convention of the association was to prepare strategy for the L.C.A. convention of July, 1972, in Dallas, which would receive the revised report from the national denominational commission and act on it. The organization circularized an advance resolution critical of the report. They then prepared an alternative paper urging a decentralized structure possessing a dual executive at both national and synodical levels: a chief pastor/theologian *assisted* by a chief administrator. And finally they prepared an approved slate of nominees for the Executive Council and several national boards.

At Dallas the restructuring that went through was limited to centralizing existing national boards. Some approved nominees were elected to national boards. But, above all, the national image of the A.L.C.P.L. was found to be changed from that of crazy radical faction, in the eyes of the general pastorate, to that of solid renewalist organization. The anomalous result is that the national bureaucrats are more impressed with the association; but less fearful of it! Thus the A.L.C.P.L. has a more recognized place at this writing, but has to work harder to accomplish lasting renewal. No one, a year previously, could have forecast this situation.

American Society of Professional Clergy (Unincorporated)

At about the same time as the dialogue in the midwest in the late 1960's which led to the founding of the Academy of Parish Clergy, a similar conversation was going on amongst some members of the Essex North Association, Massachusetts Conference, United Church of Christ. There was a desire to draw together and work for the improvement of the practice of parish ministry, as distinguished from out-of-parish continuing education efforts. What resulted was the formation of the American Society of Professional Clergy, containing a dozen and a half UCC pastors and one United Methodist minister.

The society chartered itself in the Commonwealth of Massachusetts and went to work on setting definite standards. An approach to the latter was tentatively broached which might have been unique among clergy associations: defining them *through the expectation of lay persons* towards the parish minister, and how and for what these persons were to hold him accountable. But here the forward motion stopped. A president was elected, but no statement of purpose or constitution was set up. The society was not incorporated. The Rev. A. Karl Phillippi of Georgetown, Massachusetts, holds what material and information there is in his files and answers correspondence.

Academy of Adventist Ministers (organized 1971)

Sponsored by the Ministerial Association of the General Conference of the Seventh Day Adventists, the Academy of Adventist Ministers is a voluntary, semi-official, contributory, membership organization concerned with the continuing education of ministers regardless of academic standing. Its standards of achievement for maintaining membership owe a great deal to the Academy of Parish Clergy. The standards, which are of interest, follow: 1) A member is to maintain a good and regular standing as a Seventh Day Adventist Minister; 2) he is to complete a minimum of 150 clock hours of approved continuing professional education each three years; 3) he may divide studies between work done in the church and work done away from the church; 4) he is to choose areas of study and growth on the basis of his professional needs; 5) he is to incorporate in his continuing education tangible evidence of what he has learned; 6) he is to submit his demonstration of learning to critical evaluation by a qualified peer or superior; and 7) the employing organization pays required dues annually to support the collective cause of upgrading professional competence in the ministry.

The A.A.M. works through established denominational seminary continuing education courses, a Home Study Institute, and additional field schools, extension courses, and workshops. Categories of membership are Regular, Associate, Student, and Retired. A unique characteristic of all classes of membership is that prospects must have two sponsors who are Regular members, plus two recommendations from denominational executives or seminary faculty members. The association's motto is "Deeper Commitment through Deeper Understanding," and it is designed to help pastors 1) keep growing mentally; 2) keep alive spiritually; 3) get out of the rut of administrative and pastoral duties; 4) be alert to a changing world; 5) dig more deeply into favorite studies; 6) explore freely new subject areas; 7) develop broad general fund of essential knowledge; and 8) specialize in areas needed by the church.

Due to its limited scope, dealing only with continuing education, the A.A.M. is not a fully professional clergy association or academy. But it is related to the movement and stimulated thereby, not only making use of the movement's practices and know-how but also making its own valuable contribution.

The A.A.M.'s legitimacy as a professional association or academy of clergy is further questioned because it is

organized and run from the top down. It is not a peer
support system, with the power and the structure set that
enable sharing and help on the peer level.

According to coordinator Glenn S. Sharman of the
Takoma Park Seventh Day Adventist Church in Maryland,
the Academy was voted into being by the General
Conference Ministerial Department of the denomination in
1970, organized in the fall of 1971, and promotion of the
organization began early in 1972. By mid-summer 1972,
there were 200 paid members out of a potential of 3,200.

The academy is "directed" by the General Conference
Ministerial Department. Its program is subsidized from the
denominational world budget. In some instances membership
dues are paid for the individual pastor by his local
conference. While the academy is a voluntary organization as
to membership, it seems semi-official as to financing and
direction.

College of Professional Christian Ministers (1971)

The C.P.C.M. is the most recently organized
denominational clergy association, and it is still definitely a
regional one, being an entity for Disciples of Christ ministers
in the Illinois-Wisconsin region. This is indeed a realistic level
at which to begin, for much of life beyond the local parish
level in the Disciples is carried on in the dozen-odd regions of
this national church body.

The genesis of the College was in an April, 1971, draft
paper entitled "The Dream: A New Life-Style for the
Professional Disciples Pastor" in which eight clergy called for
a regional college of pastors. This structure was to attempt to
meet a variety of 1) personal, 2) professional, and 3) political
needs, and these objects were quite openly and frankly
stated. Since then, thirteen clusters, or chapters, around

Illinois and Wisconsin have been set up, five of which are quite active. There is a dean at the head of each chapter. The deans together constitute the senate of the College of Professional Christian Ministers of Wisconsin and Illinois.

In 1972 particular projects were begun in the areas of support systems and professional identity. November of that year saw the first issue of *The Journal,* a three times a year, eight page news sheet under the editorship of David E. Goss of Bloomington, Illinois.

In 1973 there have been the formalizing of a constitution, a "covenanting service" at which members were received, and the participating in the Steering Committee of an Interfaith Coalition for Ministry (the first use of S.C.I.C.M. as a means to help a home association become national). Ahead lie the vision of combining with the other active regional Disciples ministers' group (in the greater Washington, D.C. area), and others, to form a truly national association, and the thought of official representations to the 1975 denominational assembly. But the dozen regions of the nation are conceived of as the best level at which to put major effort.

SCICM — *The Ecumenical Dimension* (1971)

By 1971 at least a few persons in key places in the clergy association/professional academy network felt there was a good deal of waste motion and parochialism. As they became aware of the mushrooming number of associations and networks, they sensed that many groups were putting much effort into learning things that were already in the experience of other going groups. Furthermore, in areas such as ethnic caucuses, college ministry, civil rights, many people found themselves closer together in mutual understanding and support than they were to persons within their own denomination. On top of this came the financial crunch of the early 1970's, coupled with the knowledge that foundation funds for new projects went first to those under ecumenical auspices or with an ecumenical aspect or impact. The Association of Episcopal Clergy, for example, had gone to the Lilly Endowment in 1970 with a proposal for a pilot national structure for research, standards, and organizing, and had been told that the idea was intriguing but they should revise it along ecumenical lines if they wished to receive substantial funds.

Accordingly, in March, 1971, the A.E.C. called an informal meeting with the Academy of Parish Clergy, the Association of Lutheran Clergy and Professional Layworkers, and the National Federation of Priests Councils at the Urban Training Center in Chicago. (Hoped-for representation from the Association of United Church Ministers and the Salvation Army did not materialize.) This conference discovered widespread agreement and defined common interests: 1) funding, 2) handling dual memberships, 3) the non-stipendiary ministry, 4) mechanics of cooperation and consultation, 5) competency and vocation, 6) viability of small parishes, 7) academic versus practical seminary training, 8) clergy surplus and shortage, and 9) identifying other areas of concern. The conference also issued a declaration addressed to all known clergy association groups, calling for the foundation of an ecumenical congress for ministry to be an umbrella for organizations of clergy associations and academies to "serve as a vehicle of communication to study, plan, organize and execute the programs of its constituents as they endeavor to evoke and express self-determination for the development and improvement of clergy in response to God's spirit at work in the world."

By September 13, 1971, there were eight groups at a second week-long session in DesPlaines, Illinois: the

Unitarian-Universalist Ministers Association, the National Network of Episcopal Clergy Associations (successor to the Association of Episcopal Clergy), the National Federation of Priests Councils (Roman Catholic), the Academy of Parish Clergy (interfaith), the Association of United Church Ministers, the Association of Lutheran Clergy and Professional Layworkers, the Union of American Baptist Clergy, and the Ministers Council American Baptist Convention. This meeting defined the purpose and style and goals of a possible network as follows:

1. Purpose: To foster interfaith communications and mutual help among clergy; to build wide support systems for membership; to augment dignity, self-esteem and personal integrity among us so we may improve our capacity to serve usefully in our religious vocation.
2. Style: To assist members of associations and academies to develop and implement strategies for the enhancement of the effectiveness in mission as appropriate to each association. Not a policy or program agency, but a communications, service and catalytic agency responsible to its member organizations.
3. Goals:
   a. To provide a communications network.
   b. To provide services in strategy development.
   c. To provide documentation to the movement.
   d. To encourage evolution of standards of competence, of professional ethics and of personnel procedures.
   e. To recruit additional associations as they come into being.

This done, the conferees set up a Steering Committee of an Interfaith Congress on Ministry (S.C.I.C.M.) and took home a proposal to their home groups that they join the steering committee, contribute towards a modest budget, use the services of Enablement, Inc. (a Boston agency serving clergy associations and the non-stipendiary ministry) for help in administration and communications, and to move into a two-year development process toward setting up a permanent national network, rather than a superassociation. Autonomy of each member organization was to be safegurded.

January, 1972, saw another Chicago meeting, with about the same number of organizations in attendance: the National Federation of Priests Councils; Society of Priests for a Free Ministry (new — see section following); Academy of Parish Clergy; Unitarian-Universalist Ministers Association; the Chicago affiliate of the National Network of Episcopal Clergy Associations; the Association of United Church Ministers; the Union of American Baptist Clergy; and Enablement, Inc., now ready to handle administrative and communication services for the network on an interim basis. The Ministers Council American Baptist Convention; the American Society of Professional Clergy (new); and a nascent Disciples group, as well as the Association of Lutheran Clergy and Professional Layworkers were unable to attend.

After a year of meetings and work, the ecumenical coalition evaluated its work, its credibility and effectiveness, set up a minimal budget and structure for 1972, and decided to continue its life and work in a more visible style. It changed its name to Steering Committee of an Interfaith *Coalition* for Ministry (still S.C.I.C.M.!).

Four groups were committed to membership, and two of them came to the conference with initial pledges for

S.C.I.C.M. financing. Four more thought they would be members by the end of the year. There were then eleven known clergy association/professional academy bodies. A year's effort had brought into being a consortium with extremely modest financing and some beginnings in communication services, joint consultation, and documentation of the association movement and its concerns. But there had not yet been sufficient investment of time, money, or structure to accomplish measurable achievements, other than a monthly newsletter, semi-annual monographs, and the basic beginnings of regular communication among the eleven organizations in the movement. The question was whether S.C.I.C.M. was a credible and effective tool worth the effort to bring it into being and maintain it. The need to answer this question was made doubly clear by a challenge from the Department of the Ministry, National Council of Churches, which had met a week before. Some members of the department regarded S.C.I.C.M. as unnecessary, others saw it as premature, and still others suggested it be replaced by a Department of the Ministry-sponsored committee consisting of a grass roots clergyman from each denominational association/professional academy, a middle management executive from each denomination, and coordinative convenorship by the National Council of Churches.

The response of the S.C.I.C.M. meeting was to declare that the coalition was much more representative and effective than anything that might arise out of denominational middle management structure or the conciliar organization; that its effectiveness and credibility had legitimately been questioned, but that the answer required sufficient time, money, and structure for the coalition to accomplish its goals. Accordingly, the statement of S.C.I.C.M.'s intentions was simplified to state that its purpose was to enhance ministry in effectiveness, relevance, and mission, and to set five tasks for the ensuing year:

1. Joint membership at reduced rates in the interfaith Academy of Parish Clergy and the denominational organizations.
2. Setting guidelines for profiles of congregations in the jurisdictions of member pastors, and the completion of such a file in a target jurisdiction.
3. Approaching specific foundations for funding experimental projects.
4. The collation of existing denominational and association codes of ethics into a suggested ecumenical code of ethics and professional standards.
5. Building up a documentation file of successful ecumenical congregations, building-sharing experiments, and ecumenical community ministries.

The rest of 1972 saw another meeting in September, with full membership taken on by the Unitarian-Universalist Ministers Association and the Society of Priests for a Free Ministry (an organization of married Latin-rite Roman Catholic priests functioning as non-stipendiary liturgists, as described below). A useful documentation packet on congregational profiles was produced, a joint membership agreement between the Academy of Parish Clergy and denominational organizations put into effect, and further plans laid. Effective January 15, 1973, S.C.I.C.M. adds a minimum of structure to its two meetings per year, with Edwin Stevens, an American Baptist pastor in Arlington Heights, Illinois, becoming chairman, and Mary Louise Schniedwind, Administrative Officer of the National Federation of Priests Councils, setting up an organizational treasury. S.C.I.C.M. continues to be a minimum-structure umbrella for sharing and communication, strategy and financial development, and documentation to the clergy association/professional academy movement.

The Society of Priests for a Free Ministry (1968-69)

A word must be added here about an organization which has just joined the coalition of clergy associations — the Society of Priests for a Free Ministry. It is both an organization of tent-makers and a clergy association, and perhaps will find its identity partly in one movement and partly in the other.

Founded by a group of married Latin-rite Roman Catholic priests who desire to continue in the active ministry in ways not yet fully clear to them, the S.P.F.M. is now officially organized, with officers, an administrative center, a newsletter, and an executive board of regional representatives. It held its third annual meeting in New York City in September, 1971, at which the presidency passed from Professor Eugene Bianchi of Emory University, Atlanta, Georgia, to Professor Bernard McGoldrick of Fresno State College, California. Their mailing list is about 1,300 persons, of which the number of married priests is estimated to be one half. There are several hundred paid-up members. Some of the latter are Catholic priests still fully within the structure, clergy and laity across the ecumenical spectrum, and sympathetic resource persons and theologians of the caliber of Dr. Rosemary Ruether and Father Gregory Baum, O.S.A. Because the active leadership of S.P.F.M. is made up of men and women of high intelligence and considerable talents, this group bears careful watching.

In its three years of life, S.P.F.M. has set up a network for mutual stimulation through the use of a newsletter, "Diaspora," as well as annual meetings and other means. It has found certain areas in which new types of ministry, while unofficial, may operate above ground and be accepted by the established religious institution. And it has achieved a breakthrough in deciding that the basic issue with which it wishes to deal is not the question of optional celibacy (which is important but secondary) but the opportunity for offering new types of ministry and priesthood which would not involve the institutional church financially. A ministry of married clergy, for example, would be unfeasible financially for the Latin-rite, western Roman Catholic Church, even if fully permissible, for some years to come, and here is a way to finance them and make them *free*. Hence the name Society of Priests for a *Free* Ministry. The ministry is done for love, not for pay, and so is free in still another sense.

The last year has seen an unsuccessful attempt to form an unofficial coalition of post-Vatican II renewalist groups, such as the S.P.F.M., the National Federation of Priests Councils, the National Association for Pastoral Renewal, the National Association for Laity, and sisters', black, and Hispanic caucuses. The Fourth annual meeting in Los Angeles joined S.C.I.C.M., and made plans to concretize opportunities for reciprocal ministerial recognition, utilize and support non-traditional forms of ministry; establish a national board of certification for skilled pastoral care specialists, community needs planners, educators, counsellors, *etc.*; develop an annual yearbook as a resource bank for emerging experimental projects; and foster de-institutionalized contract-parishes.

S.P.F.M. suffers from two handicaps, in the opinion of some observers. The first is a frustration at being unofficial and thus dealing with much smaller constituencies than members previously were able to affect through parishes and official agencies. The second is in handling necessary but secondary organizational detail. Most active members of

S.P.F.M. have found the institutional church juridical, rule-conscious, and rigid to the point of preventing effective ministry. Many of them therefore have a "thing" about organizational detail and either avoid it or tend not to follow through on it. Hence a surprising amount of organizational mistakes for such a talented group of people. This author's hope is that time will heal the hurts caused by too many rules and details, and a better, more organized approach will result.

There is no doubt, however, that the Society of Priests for a Free Ministry is a clergy association, judging by the criteria enumerated near the beginning of this chapter. It is an exemplary, sacrificial peer support group. Sharing and helping within the S.P.F.M. and with married or troubled Roman Catholic clergy is inspiring to behold. Members work on improving each other's skills, on the enablement of new and effective forms of ministry, and on ethics and standards for undertaking and upholding these. Finally, they campaign tirelessly for due process and justice from the institutional church.

Conclusions

Some random concluding observations come out of the research for this chapter and the building of files on this movement in the last two to three years.

The first comes from the experience of local and national groups in the difficult task of organizing, coming to life, being active, and rendering assistance. Sooner or later, during the period of birth and adolescence, every clergy association learns for itself in its own way that the bishop or hierarch or executive or denominational administrator is *not* the enemy. The enemy is clerical apathy. A great deal of energy can be wasted if this lesson is not taken to heart. Contrariwise, if this is recognized, a great deal of latent energy can be unleashed in giving hope and specific attainable goals to the pastor in the pulpit.

The second observation is that what characterizes a living and creative clergy association/professional academy is winning a victory on a concrete issue. For the National Federation of Priests Councils it may have been the inclusion of due process boards in the structure of many dioceses. For the Academy of Parish Clergy it may have been the actual functioning of the first colleague groups, and their effect on pastors in the community they served. For the Association of Episcopal Clergy it was the turnaround in the attitude of the Church Pension Fund. The victory animates the group from that moment on. It is no longer merely a question of lists and meetings and resolutions and plans and actions. It is a living and growing together, a sharing in order to do ministry.

The third conclusion can be termed nothing less than resurrection. Clergy associations and professional associations can and do transform men from isolated loners into disciplined, increasingly skilled, open, human, and loving parsons. I have personally seen the action of such groups draw in the clergy in the area whom I have called "walking wounded," those who had given up and settled for a bare existence on the periphery. I have seen tired, shriveled, old men stop hiding in the corner, lose much of their fear, and step forward as renewed men. I have seen their church boards exclaim, "What has happened to Parson Jones since he started going to the association?" and I trust that this movement has affected me too.

Footnotes

1. For example James O. S. Huntington, O.H.C., in the Knights of Labor in the 1880's and 1890's. See Vida Scudder's biography of Fr. Huntington, published in New York in 1940.

2. Chapter 2, *The Airline Pilots: A Study in Elite Unionization,* Cambridge, Harvard University Press, 1971.
3. *New York Times,* December 19, 1971, Sunday Travel Section.
4. I am particularly indebted for the basic ideas here to the Rev. Edward R. Sims, first President of the Washington Episcopal Clergy Association, first Chairman of the National Network of Episcopal Clergy Associations, and a skilled apologist for the movement.
5. *Ex-Pastors: Why Men Leave the Parish Ministry,* Boston, Pilgrim Press, 1970.
6. Earl Blue Associates, San Francisco; Human Resource Developers, Boston; Bearings for Re-establishment, New York.
7. The Rt. Rev. John M. Burgess of Boston at the January 3, 1973, meeting of the Massachusetts Clerical Association (not a clergy association!) at Trinity Episcopal Church, Boston.
8. New York, McKay, 1959. Especially chapters 7 and 14.
9. *WECA Newsletter,* January 1972, Vol. III, No. 5
10. The exact phrase seems to have been coined by the Rev. Edward Sims of Potomac, Maryland (*cf.* footnote 4, this chapter).
11. Cf. Introduction to *Worldly Goods* by James Gollin, New York, Random House, 1971. Also *Documents of Vatican II,* general editor Walter M. Abbot, S.J., New York; Guild, American and Association Presses, 1966.
12. *Priests-USA,* November, 1971; National Federation of Priests Councils, p.6.
13. *Why National Federation of Priests Councils,* 2nd edition, February 1971, by Frank Bonnike.
14. According to the *National Catholic Reporter.*
15. *Cf.* page 4, *Why N.F.P.C.* (footnote 13).
16. *Priests-USA;* February 1971, and contemporary issues of *National Catholic Reporter.*
17. *N.F.P.C. newsletter,* June 1970.
18. He is now President of Lancaster Theological Seminary, Lancaster, Pennsylvania.
19. Abingdon Press, Nashville and New York; 1968.
20. *Authority and Power in the Free Church Tradition,* Princeton and London, Princeton and Oxford University Presses, 1959 and 1960.
21. *Tomorrow,* M and M Benefits Board of American Baptist Convention, May, 1969, p. 3 ff.

National Clergy Association/Professional Academy Groups, Spring, 1973
[* indicates Communicator]

1. Academy of Parish Clergy — interfaith professional academy; * Executive Secretary — Ms. Phyllis Byers, 3100 West Lake Street, Minneapolis, Minnesota 55416. Editor, Journal of the APC — Dr. Robert W. Croskery, First Congregational Church, 2315 Collingwood, Toledo, Ohio 43620.
2. National Federation of Priests Councils (Roman Catholic); President — the Rev. Reid Mayo, 1307 South Wabash Avenue, Chicago, Illinois 60605. Administrative Officer — Mary Louise Schniedwind, same address. * Communicator — the Rev. Frank Brown, same address.

3. National Network of Episcopal Clergy Associations; Chairman — the Rev. Edward R. Sims, 318 E. Fourth St., Cincinnati, Ohio 45202. * Communicator — the Rev. Claudius Miller, III, 1166 South Mason Road, St. Louis, Missouri 63131.

4. American Society of Professional Clergy — mostly U.C.C. plus one United Methodist; * the Rev. A. Karl Phillippi, 12 West Main Street, Georgetown, MA 01830.

5. Association of United Church Ministers; * Coordinator — the Rev. J. Robert Zinn, 20 North Elmwood Avenue, Waukegan, Illinois 60085.

6. Unitarian-Universalist Ministers Association; President — the Rev. Leon Fay, 13454 Desert Hills N.E., Albuquerque, New Mexico 87111. * Communicator — the Rev. Bruce Clary, 25 Orange Street, Barre, Vermont 05641. Office work — the Rev. George Spencer, Unitarian-Universalist Association, 25 Beacon Street, Boston, MA 02108.

7. Association of Lutheran Clergy and Professional Layworkers (L.C.A.): President — Pastor Robert Ruble, 32 South Fifth Street, Allentown, Pennsylvania 18101. * A.L.C.P.I. Newsletter, 517 Sangree Road, Pittsburgh, Pa. 15237 (the Rev. Richard Dowhower).

8. Union of American Baptist Clergy, Inc.; * President and Communicator — the Rev. Richard Bowser, Union of American Baptist Clergy, First Baptist Church, Granville, Ohio 43023. Newsletter Editor — the Rev. Robert Noblett, 20110 Lorain Road, Apt. 517, Fairview Park, Ohio 44126.

9. Ministers Council, American Baptist Convention, * Executive Director — the Rev. Charles N. Fosberg, American Baptist Convention, Valley Forge, Pennsylvania 19481.

10. Academy of Adventist Ministers; * Coordinator — the Rev. Glenn S. Sharman, 6951 Carroll Ave., Takoma Park, Washington, D.C. 20012.

11. Society of Priests for a Free Ministry; President — Bernard McGoldrick, 515 East Menlo, Fresno, California 93715. * Office — Robert Duryea, 16788 Littlefield Lane, Los Gatos, California 95030.

12. College of Professional Christian Ministers (Disciples of Christ—Illinois and Wisconsin): President—Roger A. Zollars, 310 S. Main St., Edwardsville, Illinois 62025; Communicator—David Goss, First Christian Church, 401 Jefferson Ave., Bloomington, Illinois 61701.

CHAPTER FOUR

Non-Viabilility

In the fast-changing, exciting, but threatening world we live in, one problem affecting the church in general and the clergy in particular has been what we have analyzed as a leadership vacuum at the top. A second problem for local clergy has been the non-viability of local ministry units. We seem to have too many, too-small congregations properly to support full time clergy with proper equipment to do an adequate Christian work.

Small Congregations

In days of yore, a greater percentage of resources was concentrated at the local level. The average main line Christian pastor had an education superior to nearly everyone in town. In the days before the emergence of many specialized professions in the nineteenth century,[1] the local pastor had more graduate education than the local school superintendent; more canon law (and thus jurisprudence) training than the local attorney, who most likely had only done an apprenticeship in his uncle's office; and more medical knowledge than the local sawbones, through the church's experience with psychosomatic healing, exorcism, and hospitals, while surgery had not yet been fully separated from barbering. This is to say that in the old days, the rectory or parsonage was the number one resource center in the entire town for dealing with almost the whole range of problems of life and death. It is also to say that there was a consequent lack of need to send as much money and resources out of the local parish as is necessary in the day of the global village. Thus a congregation of fifty families or one hundred adult communicants could realistically expect to provide a secure, if not affluent, living to a pastor, maintain a church hall and parsonage, and support the home and foreign missionary work of Christianity. But the present situation is radically different.

In the mid-1960's (which I take to be the most prosperous period of the post-World War II era, ecclesiastically speaking), the outside demand, in the case of my own denomination, was for thirty per cent of a local congregation's operating money to be sent outside the local scene. (But the situation at that time was of a continuing decline in the percentage actually being remitted to regional, national, and international church purposes.)[2] A more solid cause of the new situation is the rising amount of money needed to maintain a minimal, let alone an effective, parish program. This amount grew enormously, compared to previous centuries. A key study done for the Presbytery of Manhattan in the early 1960's found that in its jurisdiction a minimal program could be mounted for $11,000 to $12,000 per year by starving the pastor and letting the buildings go to rack and ruin, that a rise in budget to $18,000 to $20,000 per year simply made for a decent minimal effort, and that a congregation could be serious about doing some work only by beginning at the latter figure. A subsequent study of the 1967-68 statistics in the Episcopal Church[3] (that was my denomination's plushest post-World War II year) set the figure for minimal effectiveness at $20,000 per year, which meant 200 communicants or 100 pledging units at current average giving rates. In 1968, 62.5 per cent of the local churches were below that line, requiring the services of 43 per cent of the active clergy to serve 18 per cent of the denominational constituency. Subsequent investigation has raised the minimum figure in the early 1970's to $25,000, which would require 125 pledging units or 250 communicants, by my rough rule of thumb for gauging such matters. And the crowning blow is the statement of a consultant active in parish development that if one's sights are raised to aim at decent financial support of the clergy, equipment well maintained, and striving for giving as much outside as inside the congregation, then $40,000 to $50,000 is the needed budgetary minimum, which means 450 communicants and 225 pledging units. But only one-fourth of the congregations have budgets of $45,000 and above, and only one-fourth of them have 440 communicants or more.[4]

Certain conclusions are obvious from the above statistics. In one denomination, the Episcopal, which is by no means atypical, 43 per cent of the clergy are serving 18 per cent of the people in 62 per cent of the parishes in a situation which is programmed for failure, which is not even above the line of minimum viability. It is a denomination, contrary to surface impression, of small congregations — too many too-small ones.

Serving congregations in a situation programmed for failure, or survival and nothing more, is a forty-year, life-time career for many of those 43 per cent of the clergy. A study of a goodly number of biographies in *The Episcopal Clergy Directory* leads me to the tentative conclusion that there are two definite career tracks for service in the Anglican church in the United States. Either one departs the below-200-communicant-and-$20,000 scene within two to three years of ordination, never to return, or else one stays in that slot most or all of one's active ministry. I would make an educated guess that one-third of the Episcopal clergy, a sizable portion, can expect to spend all of their clerical lives in congregations too small to be viable — all the more so with the contemporary clergy surplus experienced in the Episcopal Church, Unitarian-Universalist Association, and other denominations. And I would estimate the too many too-small church situation to be true in the Episcopal, United Church of Christ, American Baptist, Unitarian-Universalist denominations, and increasing in the Lutheran and Presbyterian denominations in certain parts of the country.

An Extreme Case

One extreme instance may be found in Washington County, New York, which is between the upper Hudson River near Glens Falls, and the Vermont state line. This county of 48,000 persons[5] is the only remaining undeveloped rural sector of the area surrounding the Albany-Glens Falls metropolitan area in upstate New York. Its growth projection from 1970 to 1980 is less than two per cent, in a nation expecting to grow over ten times that amount. Of fifty-seven counties in the state, it is fifty-fourth in geographic mobility and forty-eighth in in-migration.

As the same time, Washington County is one of the most highly churched counties in the nation, both in congregations per unit of population and in percentage of persons claiming church allegiance.[6] There are eighty-nine recognized congregations in a population of 48,476, or one church for every 544 people in the county. While 60.6 per cent of the population are recorded as adult members on the registers of congregations, over 85 per cent of the people claim a definite church allegiance.

Furthermore, the county is economically well below the

norm. In 1966, a prosperous year, twenty-two per cent of the families fell below the poverty line as set by the Office of Economic Opportunity. As against a national unemployment rate of four per cent, the figure in the county stood at seven per cent. The county per capita income is also below normal.

In this setting, there is one Roman Catholic Church for every 860 adults, and one non-Roman Catholic Church for every 213 adults. The per capita giving in these latter seventy-three congregations was $42.00 per annum, not including extra capital funds. There are eight Episcopal churches in the county,[7] serving a total of 946 adult members (communicants) with a per capita giving of $50.17 per annum, and employing six priests. Annual budgets in the parishes without resident priests run from $541.00 to $2,000.00, and in the congregations with resident priests, from $5,000.00 to $11,300.00. (Note that these are the closest figures available to 1967-68 which we have determined was the most prosperous post-war year for the denomination.)

While it is an extreme situation, it is not out of line with that in almost half of the local church units in the nation. Under these circumstances, anything above maintenance and minimal activities in a miracle!

Results

The results of trying to serve these numbers of non-viable congregations with as many full time pastors as possible in a full set of buildings are a concentration on the survival and maintenance role of the congregation to the exclusion of the pastoral and missionary roles; a deprivation of identity among the clergy; a consequent negative image; and an overall frustration.

The experience of executives and leaders of my

denomination is that most of the congregations that could be closed were shut during the depression of the 1930's. Those churches now left can and will survive. The good folk therein are positive geniuses at hanging on by their fingernails, and surviving — and little or nothing more! Thus the institution-survival role of the church, squeezes out the nurture-pastoral role, and the apostolic-missionary role, to use the terminology of church life developed by Joseph Fichter, the great religious sociologist.[8]

The keep-the-ship-afloat action is so all-pervasive as to render all but impossible the train-the-crew action and the chart-where-we-are-going and whom-we-are-helping action. A brief participation in the life of many of these congregations, scattered across the land, gives one the impression of desperation, financial crunch, how will we survive? and to heck with anyone outside unless they will help us!

This is not Christianity. The result may be a tight little family, friendly among itself, but it is not the Christian body at work converting the world and sanctifying souls.

Another result of non-viability is being deprived of identity, both for the clergy and lay people involved. The literature shows the acute deprivation present in these areas, negatively affecting the identity of the parson.[9]

Worth special mention is identity deprivation in the work role. We have mentioned before the pastor being the man-of-many-talents of the town in years before. But now people go to the social worker, the probation officer, the school guidance counsellor, the lawyer, and the doctor, and more often than not avoid the non-viable church pastor. This author remembers the shock he received when he, an experienced and highly trained man in the field of alcohol problems, first found such family-oriented conflicts being presented to the high school guidance counsellor, who was completely at sea in dealing with them. The point is that much of the parson's weekday pastoral work role has been taken from him.

There is also an institutional identity deprivation. The clergyman, a symbolic person, is seen as necessary for laying the wreath on the pedestal of the statue on Memorial Day, and for starting the PTA Meeting with an invocation. The church institution is seen as social glue, sticking us to the past or the eternal, and less and less a moral force and arbiter in the red-hot now, or as a first fruits of the Kingdom to come. All of this makes the identity of the parson less sure.

The consequent negative image of the church is hardly surprising. It might be pictured as a building with a water boy (wearing a clerical collar) attached. And it is the responsibility of that water boy to do the work of the church. Thus it was to my surprise in one pastorate carried on in the non-viable setting that I found I could not raise a minimal number of persons for the housekeeping and Sunday School jobs — the work necessary to maintain the fabric and do the busy work of the parish — but that the church people could be persuaded to do a great deal of work in the secular community, forming a convalescent home, working on a visiting nurse association, getting community development projects going. Indeed, they could be taught to see this as a basic part of their Christian vocation. This outreach was exciting and valuable. But in the clutches of a negative image, the people could not do the basics of church work which would prepare the next generation for this outreach. The importance of outreach was recognized, but the inner workings necessary to make the outreach deep were not.

All this adds up to a vast frustration. Lay people spend huge amounts of their time and effort on rummage sales and auctions and raffles to raise money to keep the creaking ship afloat, but are tired out when the time comes for prayer and worship, study and nurture, calling and visiting, and evangelistic outreach. The clergyman has to fill the gaps, spends most of his time doing the layman's work, neglecting the work he was particularly trained for. Everyone is frustrated. No one is happy. The proper work is not done. And the church is not fulfilling its basic function of bringing man and vision of God together.

Paradox

The strange fact is that many people in main line denominations like the size of the local ministry unit that is too small to be viable! According to Dr. H. Boone Porter, a man who in recent years has been particularly concerned with both non-metropolitan ministries and self-supporting ministries, a solid chunk of the church population in the Episcopal Church prefers life in the small congregation of roughly 150-200 adult communicants.[10] Porter's contention is that underground churches prefer an even smaller group, the United Church of Christ also a smaller number, and Roman Catholics and Baptists (where possible) prefer larger numbers for their basic ministry units. Thus the paradoxical situation is that many people prefer the size of a congregation which is too small to be viable, yet they are tense over the resulting financial, psychological, and programatic crunch.

This preference for the smaller size of local ministry may be a hint towards a way out of the problem. Perhaps it can overcome opposition to a change either in the full time status of the clergyman or the manner of his remuneration. For a look in these directions, we move onto the next chapter.

Footnotes

1. Lowery, James L., Jr., "The Clergy, The Professional, and Preparation for Ordained Ministry," *St. Luke's Journal of Theology,* Sewanee, Tenn.; Part I, Vol. XIV, No. 4, Sept. 1971 pp. 49*ff.;* Part II, Vol. XV, No. 1, Jan. 1972, pp. 58*ff.*

2. The Episcopal Church's statistics show, when one adds in the additional capital and outside expenditures, beyond normal budgeting, that the percentage of money given beyond the parish has declined from 28% in 1920 to 17% in 1967.

3. Lowery, James L., Jr., *Small Congregations and their Clergy,* January, 1970. Available from Enablement, Inc., 8 Newbury St., Boston, Mass. 02116.

4. Baxter, T. Chester, "No Wonder We're Hurting," *Episcopalian,* May, 1970, page 8.

5. Lowery, James L., Jr., "Washington County, New York; Too Many Too-Small Churches," Harvard Divinity School course monograph, Feb. 1969, p. 9 Available from Enablement, Inc. (see footnote 3).

6. a. Tennies, Arthur, "Statistical Reports prepared for a Washington County Planning Workshop," N.Y. State Council of Churches, 1968.
   b. Moore, Joseph (ed.), "Area and Church Survey for the Episcopal Diocese of Albany, N.Y.," Unit of Research and Field Survey, Episcopal Church, 1955.
   c. Ryan, Nancy, "Some facts about Washington County," Washington County Office of Economic Opportunity, 1968.

7. Lowery, "Washington County," page 17.

8. Fichter, Joseph H., S.J., *Religion as an Occupation;* University of Notre Dame Press, 1961.

9. See particularly the unpublished lectures of William B. Easter, Resources Center for Parish Clergy, Lubbock, Texas; also the book, *The Vanishing Parson* (Beacon, 1971) by Laile Bartlett.

10. Dr. Porter, after some years as a liturgics professor at Nashotah House and then the General Theological Seminary, is currently director of Roanridge Institute, 9200 NW Skyview Ave., Kansas City, Missouri 64154.

CHAPTER FIVE

Tents

Again a quiet, growing movement abroad among clergy may offer a solution: tentmaker priests and ministers.

We have seen the situation in many denominations of too many too-small ministry units on the local scene. The size of the local congregation that is the norm is below the level at which there can be a properly supported, ordained, professional staff, and a properly equipped church, parish house, and rectory/parsonage.

One possibility in this dilemma is to forego the building of a church edifice. Christ Church Presbyterian, Burlington, Vermont, refused to build a church but stayed in its multi-purpose building, formerly a radio repair shop, freeing itself financially so that its fifty families could be a lively worship unit, a series of Bible study groups, and the progenitor of multiple mission task forces. Its life and ministry bear testimony that this is an option, at least where one is not already stuck with all the buildings and cannot sell them!

Another option is not to have a full-time pastor. This can be done by having one man simultaneously serve several cures. It can also be done by having a pastor earn part or all of his living secularly. St. Paul did so. Let us look at this latter arrangement in some detail.

Free ministry, self-supporting priesthood, tentmakers, auxiliary priests, non-stipendiary ministry, supplementary ministry, voluntary priests — these are all different names used for what is essentially the same thing. An ordained person earns all or most of his bread from secular sources and performs ministry for free or for expenses. That this kind of ministry is increasing rapidly is indicated in a study which shows that, in the Episcopal Church alone, 1,300 to 2,000 of the active Episcopal clergy in the United States (out of a total active number of more than 9,000), receive over half their total compensation from secular sources.[1] (This one-half figure for compensation marks the study's definition of a non-stipendiary ministry.)

It is my contention that tentmaker ministries can make a unique contribution in our era to the practice of ministry. Furthermore, in some cases they can make viable a resident pastorate, which most Christians desire.

Ways Looked At By The Powers That Be

There are three ways that free ministries or self-supporting priesthoods are looked at by the hierarchy. First, they may be seen as underground, secret, and irregular. It is worth adding at this point that such ministries are more overt all the time. For example, Dr. Emma Lou Benignus, a professor trained in group dynamics and pastoral theology, while at the Episcopal Theological School in Cambridge, Massachusetts, spent many of her weekends and much other time off with underground groups who wanted professional help in establishing their identity and finding their mission.[2]

Second, free ministries may be viewed by the powers that be as above ground but unofficial. Progressive church executives may tolerate them in order to see what can be learned from such experimentation. Less progressive and more Machiavellian persons may see that it is best to leave these ministries alone lest they grow even faster!

A third attitude is to make the ministry official. There are several hundred married deacons trained and ordained by the Roman Catholic Church in this country now. Their ordained ministry is part time and they earn a living secularly. The Lutheran Church in American in March, 1971, issued through its Executive Council a series of guidelines that recognized and encouraged such supplementary ministries. For the L.C.A., such ministries are legitimate as long as they are not undertaken in order to avoid facing such problems as overchurched areas, undersized congregations, *etc.*

In the Episcopal Church, the Canons were changed in 1969 and 1970 to legalize and encourage tentmaking ministries. There is now a caucus of tentmaking clergy in the Episcopal Church, who work more and more in coalition with the professional clergy associations and a new non-metropolitan caucus in that denomination.

Ways The Institution Is Seen

We have described ways the institution sees the free ministers. Conversely, there are several ways the ecclesiastical institution and its executives are looked upon by the tentmakers.

The first attitude towards the institution is to be all for it just as it is. The "rear-viewer," to be described below, has no intention of changing the ecclesiastical structure or trying anything new. He is simply marking time until he can re-enter the structure as a full-time professional pastor.

The second approach is to seek to change the institution. Thus, in the Roman Catholic Church in America, the Society of Priests for a Free Ministry seeks to change official policy to enable a married, non-stipendiary, Western, Latin-rite priesthood to experiment with new forms and situations of ministry.

A third stance is anti-institutional. This approach is hostile towards the institution, and would like to do away with it. At their most negative, the works of James Kavanaugh, William DuBay, and Charles Davis approximate this approach.

A fourth atttitude towards the institution is that the persons in tentmaking ministry "couldn't care less" about it. They simply disregard the church as institution and deal only with her as the People of God and the Mystical Body of Christ in action and living wherever they happen to be. This approach is quite typical of some of the underground churches and groups nowadays.

Relation to Secular Work

There are two ways in which free or tentmaking ministries are related to the secular work performed.[3] First, one may relate one's ministry to a cluster of secular tasks which are definitely below the full vocational spectrum of one's abilities, as in the case of the classic French worker priest on the factory production line. Second comes fulfilling one's ministry by work requiring the full extent of one's skills and capabilities, such as through the positions of social worker, social services administrator, teacher, personnel officer, *etc.*

It is the opinion of this author that if the desired effect is impact on the secular structure through activities beyond the work itself, the first way is best chosen. If the desire is for time and energy left over for ecclesiastical work as such, the first way is also wise to choose. But if the end in view is the combination of secular work as a positive function of creative ministry, and an ecclesiastical function as another part of the same ministry, then the second way offers the more opportunity. Examples which may prove illuminating follow in due course.

Background

Before proceeding further, it may be well to consider the historical background of these ministries. They traditionally date from St. Paul, who financed much of his missionary journeying, as well as meeting many potential converts, by earning his living as a tentmaker. Such self-support is still the norm in many sects. It need not be considered a second class ministry, even in the main line churches where it is again coming to the fore. In the Middle Ages, support of a clergyman very often came from the Parson's Glebe — land whose harvest paid for the support of the clergyman. The clergyman himself, in many cases, tilled this land for his own support and/or that of his parish. In Colonial Virginia, the pay of the rector was in bales of tobacco, in some cases from the land of parishioners and in others from the Parson's Glebe. Such arrangements in main line churches still continue. A case in point is the Reverend Truman Heminway, rector of the Episcopal church and priest-farmer of Sherburne, Vermont, who died as recently as the mid-1950's. Father Heminway was made famous by a biography in the "Builders for Christ" series produced by Dr. H. Boone Porter. The classical theological background for the modern revival of such ministries comes from Roland Allen, author, among other works, of *Missionary Methods: St. Paul's or Ours,* now available in an inexpensive paperback.[4] Allen was an Anglican priest who served in China, England, and finally Kenya. His work recognized that the success of early Christian mission work was due in great part to locally chosen, apostolically licensed, non-professional, residentiary, local ministry which avoided paternalism, institutional investment and dependency on foreign funds.

It must also be remembered that in certain traditional areas, receiving outside income and carrying on a tentmaking ministry has always been accepted. Cases in point are teaching, the lecture circuit, writing, *etc.*

Two Types

Tentmaking ministries may be divided into two types: 1) those involving graduate seminary-trained persons who then find a secular way of earning a living; and 2) those involving locally-trained non-seminary graduates, ordained in place, and who may actually be chosen by local people. It is worth bearing in mind that the Anglican Dioceses of Hong Kong, Idaho, California, and Southwark are *dependent* on such "auxiliary clergy" for the functioning of their dioceses and aim at making such clergy arrangements a norm. Hong Kong especially intends most of its clergy to be non-stipendiary.

The Seminary-Trained

The first instance of the seminary-trained type of free ministry is the *drop-out.* He has not resigned his clerical function nor been deposed, but he has lost his interest in formal religion. His excitements are his martinis and his family. He may, on occasion, take a service or a Sunday supply assignment as a personal favor to a pastor or archdeacon or bishop who is a friend from days gone by and who is in desperate need of a "mass priest," but the ministering has little meaning to him in itself.

The second type of seminary-trained tentmaker is the *new layman.* He is similar to the drop-out in that he lets his ecclesiastical function fall into disuse while neglecting to resign it. But he is far from turning away from the church and religion. He has simply found out how wonderful it is to be a Christian person (layman) who lives ministry and liturgy in this way, especially in the job he does for remuneration. Faith and work are very closely linked for him. He, too, occasionally functions as an ecclesiastic. An example is Dr. Meryl Ruoss, a Presbyterian minister who teaches the planning process to church people, community development workers, businessmen, *etc.*, as Professor of Urban Ecology at the University of Southern California. He is a dedicated Christian, competent and caring, and he has a genuine, conscious ministry, but in the sense that any Christian can have a real ministry. He is less and less exercising any ecclesiastical function.

A third type of seminary-trained person is the *rear-viewer*. He would go back to the old-style ministry at the first opportunity, but personal situations, marriage situations, financial problems, or the growing clergy surplus in some main line denominations have put him temporarily in a situation of earning his living in a secular job. He functions as a parish pastor when he can and looks for the first chance to return to his former position. There are, for example, a considerable number of these men in the Chicago area of the Episcopal Church, who have found there an official liaison with the full-time ministry through the help of William Maxwell, Dean of the Chicago cathedral.

A fourth type of seminary-trained free minister is the *moonlighter*. He spends a minor part of his time at a secular endeavor, but this work brings him the majority of his income and is a real ministry. Father David Randles of St. George's Episcopal Church, Clifton Park, outside Schenectady, New York, often serves as a state-appointed mediator and fact-finder assigned to certain kinds of public employment negotiatons at $100 per day. (He does *not* receive the majority of his income thus, but it is a logical extension of his ministry.) Father Neil Stanley, late rector of St. Andrew's Episcopal Church, Denver, Spent a certain amount of his time writing dime novels a generation ago, and the income from this supported his salary and a major portion of the parish budget. My own boss, when I worked for the Association of Episcopal Clergy, was the Reverend John T. Whiston, a parish priest in California with a Ph.D. in psychology. He put in ten hours a week as a state-licensed family-life counsellor in a medical clinic, at the request of the doctors. This work provided him the majority of his income. This work clearly constitutes a ministry in a secular setting.

A fifth instance to be noted is the *pigeonholer,* who lives in the secular world five days a week and enjoys a job which constitutes a real ministry. He serves the ecclesiastical world evenings and Sundays in a satisfying church position, no longer involving worries about plumbing and organs breaking down! However, his two functions are unrelated. A case in point is the Southern Pacific yard boss in El Paso, Texas, who also served as assistant priest at St. Alban's Episcopal Church in that city in the early 1950's.

The sixth type of seminary-trained free ministry I refer to rather loosely as the *non-stipendiary ministry.* Its essence is one ministry in two functions. There is a clergyman in California who is the town healer both as medical practitioner and Presbyterian pastor. In Dorchester, Massachusetts, there was Bill Manseau, minister extraordinary, who at one time functioned as a Model Cities executive by day and as a eucharistiser and counsellor by night and on weekends. He left to begin an exciting ecumenical experiment in Dunstable, Middlesex County, as "Ecumenical

Pastor" of a Congregational church though he was a *Roman Catholic priest.* The gain ecumenically, it seems to me, was a loss to the tentmaking ministry.

Another of this type is David Weyrich of Columbus, Ohio, who before ordination was a manager in a large complex of laundry and cleaning establishments. He has one ministry now — to the southern white Appalachians who stream to Columbus and other cities and have trouble finding jobs because of their lack of skills and education, and who find no meaning in the strange new urban world. But David does this in his ecclesiastical function as Rector of St. John's Episcopal Church and his secular function as assistant manager of an Armenian rug emporium and rug cleaning establishment, twenty-one of whose twenty-two employees are southern hillbillies. He spends thirty to thirty-five hours a week as assistant manager and twenty to twenty-five hours as rector. He lives in the west side area where both his church and business are situated. Much of the work he does serves both functions at once. His boss is pleased to have a skilled man bringing order out of cost-accounting chaos, and he is just as pleased at the manpower retraining program David is bringing to the business, making his labor force more skilled and finding the money for much of the retraining through Federal funds. The parish is no longer on the dole but fully self-supporting, since it pays the rector only $5,000 plus pension. There is parish money left over each year for the first time in its history. After an epic struggle, the surplus went into mission funds outside, plus the emergency food pantry and furniture exchange the parish runs for newly arrived Appalachians. This "epic struggle" is a sign of something else exciting. The parish can now afford to fight, to face, and to resolve its conflicts. Before, parishioners feared that the slightest struggle would drive away their pastor. And previous clergy hated to work on changes involving struggle because the least lowering of giving would mean extinction. The combined salaries and allowances have allowed David to buy his own home in the area, giving him an equity for the future. The parish is freed up for change and growth and mission. A business can "do well by doing good," to quote Tom Lehrer. And it is one ministry in two functions, with the clergyman time and time again finding one action serves both functions at once.

Still another example is to be seen in what this author might have done in his last pastoral cure, if only he had had the wisdom and strength. I served two small congregations which together were barely able to provide the minimum clergy salary. They did practically nothing together, since the people in the two communities had little in common. In the larger parish, many problems, especially in the field of alcohol abuse, were dealt with by the high school guidance man rather than myself. Oddly enough, he was unskilled in these areas and swamped by the demands, while I was highly experienced and trained. What transpired was a rather rueful comedy. By keeping my ears to the ground, I would know who was seeing Mr. Guidance. I would check with him on the problem. If it was beyond both of us, I would go to the case-work agency maintained by our diocese in Albany for expert help. They would teach me how to deal with it. I would then teach Mr. Guidance how to deal with it.

How much better it would have been for me to have been, at one and the same time, the resident pastor in the one town twenty hours a week and the high school guidance counsellor forty hours a week. The schedules could have dovetailed; I have accreditation in both fields; and there would have been one ministry — family pastoral counsellor — in two functions, one secular and the other ecclesiastical.

The seventh and final type of seminary-trained free minister is the *worker-priest,* whether on the classic French Roman Catholic model or the English Anglican model pioneered by David Edwards and others. Here one works, earns one's bread, and has one's total ecclesiastical ministry, all in and to the secular structure. An American case in point is that of Dick Dunne of Chicago, who resigned as radio-TV man for the Church Federation of Greater Chicago in order to become a private, for-profit, radio-TV consultant, as well as master of ceremonies on "The Action People" on educational television for the Stone-Brandell Foundation. He feels it is vitally important that he is doing this as an ordained Presbyterian minister in the secular media setting, but equally important that his ministry is full-time in that communications structure.

The Locally-Trained

The other type of free minister is the non-seminary one. This is the local person with 1) character, 2) communication skills, 3) leadership ability, and 4) saleable secular skills, who is a part-time priest and pastor or else a part-time specialist assistant priest, who is trained and ordained in place and who agrees to remain in the locality.

Within the locally trained ministry, I see two types defined by skills. The first is a man with a saleable skill and place in the community already formed, such as the sanitation engineer in a growing section of Kowloon who becomes, after due training, an auxiliary priest of the Anglican Diocese of Hong Kong. A second is the man who needs training in a skill and time in order to become established in the community. A case in point is a man from a South Shore community near Boston. He has already gone for training to gain accreditation as a high school social studies teacher, with ecclesiastical financial help. He will then teach in the school system, and on the side study for ordination, after which he will be youth-minister to the local community, both as a full-time teacher and as a part-time educational assistant with a local congregation (with the full approval and joint connivance of the school superintendent of the community and the pastor of the congregation).

The second type of the locally trained sort of tentmaker is defined by the *method of selection* used.[5] The first group of these are the *self-selected*, who come, with little or much theological and Biblical training, as the case may be, and offer themselves for the ministry. An example is the Reverend Guy Kagey of Arlington, Vermont, a retired Air Force officer, accredited elementary and secondary teacher of retarded students, Deputy Sheriff of Bennington County, expert in alcohol problems, and priest of the Episcopal Diocese of Albany in charge of Trinity Church, Whitehall, New York. Another group are those identified and selected *by a recruiting ecclesiastical authority*, such as in the plan proposed for the Western Kentucky ministry out of Owensboro in the Episcopal Diocese of Kentucky. Still another group are those identified, elected, partly trained by, and presented for ordination by, *the local people of God.* This latter type I take to be the one most fully in consonance with the teachings of Roland Allen and most fully approaching the practice of the apostolic and sub-apostolic Christian church, which was so manifestly successful; it also seems to be the rarest!

Some interesting guidelines have been developed in selecting men for such ministries. The sole insistence in Hong Kong is that the man already be operating at the professional level and that he be a man of devotion. More detailed guidelines developed in Idaho insist that the locally-trained minister be 1) settled with some prospect of permanence; 2) have demonstrated devotion, ability and leadership capabilities; 3) that he be emotionally quite stable; and 4) that he have a strong, tested marriage able to stand the double time-demand. The married Roman Catholic deacons must have the written permission of their wives in order to be accepted for ordination and training.

Another lesson from the Idaho experience is the development of some area ministries with team-staff (somewhat akin to the co-pastorates being tried out in slightly different settings in some Roman Catholic dioceses). In Idaho, teams are made up of a lay evangelist, an auxiliary priest, and a professional full-time priest, and the team together runs as one entity a large multi-parish unit.

The Criterion for Creativeness

After looking at the mushrooming movement for free ministries or self-supporting priesthoods, after reviewing its historical background and the various attitudes of the hierarchy toward it, and after isolating various types of such ministries, it occurs to this commentator that certain of them represent approaches unique to our age. St. Paul's tentmaking was pursued in order to finance his missionary tours and as a way to meet people in the marketplace. But in our century the secular function and the ecclesiastical function do not necessarily conflict and can not only complement one another but in fact constitute *one ministry*. In such cases, the minister is not split down the middle by two separate demands on his time. This can happen, as we have seen, in the case of the seminary-trained moonlighter who is a reconciler both as a pastor and state-assigned mediator for certain labor disputes in Schenectady, New York. It is of the essence for the non-stipendiary seminary-trained man and the seminary-trained worker-priest. And it can happen in the locally-trained situation with careful preparation and development. A case in point is lawyer Bob Sharp, who practices criminal law in Kansas City, Kansas, and serves an area parish. He finds that much of his pastoral counselling comes through his law office, and that his law office is a helpful adjunct to his parish work. The two interpenetrate. And how important such a way of doing things is for a denomination, such as my own Episcopal Church, which in its most affluent year found 62.5 per cent of its congregations with budgets below $21,000 and fewer than 200 communicants.[6] I suspect the situation is similar in several other denominations.

The Criterion for Liveability

The question arises of being able to survive, much less to be creative, while being active in two or three places at once. There is a way to do so, which I call the "criterion for liveability" and which was developed by Dr. H. Boone Porter.

According to Dr. Porter, a non-stipendiary or tentmaker may be involved in as many as three different places: residence, work, and church position. If these three are separate, the result will prove intolerable. If two of the three can be in the same place, the situation is bearable to good. And if all three are carried on in the same area or neighborhood, the situation is excellent and pregnant with possibilities.

Following this criteria, David Weyrich, mentioned above as a "non-stipendiary type," worked first to get his job and his church position located in the same west side of Columbus, Ohio. But there were still some strong tensions. He finally sold his home in the suburbs and purchased an old house on the west side and found having residence, secular work, and ecclesiastical position in the same area made his whole ministry jell in a new and marvelous mannner.

A slightly different case is that of Donald Cutler, who owns his own home in Westchester County, New York, is priest-in-charge of a parish nearby, and half-time literary agent in New York City. The church-and-job "thing" comes together through his projects in the field of publishing books with religious concern (a field he is well-versed in after acting as religion editor of the Beacon Press and Harper and Row). But the thing that presently fascinates Cutler the most is having his parish-and-residence combination separate from his secular work. He is learning to live, as do most of the males in his parish, the split life of work in one place and residence in another, sharing with his parishioners the dichotomy between the world of endeavor and the world of personal concerns. His men live in both worlds and seek ways to be Christians in both. Cutler's present situation gives him a way to share such a life and to work knowledgeably at ministering to it. This comes, in part, because two of the three places of action are joined together — an interesting extension of the criterion of liveability.

The Criterion for Targetability

Another way to analyze tentmaking ministries is in terms of how effectively focused they are on target.[7] Possible targets for ministry are 1) within a congregation or parish, 2) an entire community, and 3) a secular structure.

If the point of the secular job is to enable a congregation to exist in mission, then the filling of the secular position will be done in a manner to leave opportunities for meeting parish emergencies, for example. But if the target of a secular position and an ecclesiastical ministry is the humanization of a community, a different organization will be necessary. And if the focus of a combined ministry is a secular structure, such as a resort area, still another style would be necessary. The ultimate criterion is keeping the ministry focused on the target area, and knowing what that area is.

The Criterion for Beginning Such a Ministry

A final criterion for use in undertaking tentmaking ministries is beginning them only with acknowledged authority in the community. The key to the successful beginning of a tentmaking ministry is that the clergyman involved must already have status in and acceptance by the local community.[8] This factor cannot be too highly emphasized. If the person is already known as a man of character and skill, to whom the community may turn, there is much less difficulty in beginning a tentmaking ministry. If the person, however, is an unknown quantity, as well as attempting a new and different type of ministry and life-style, he will have two strikes against him at the very outset.

This introduces two options. One is beginning a ministry within the ecclesiastical structure and continuing on this base alone, as did David Weyrich in Columbus, until such time as he was established. Then the tentmaker finds a secular position that will mesh with his church position, and only at this point attempts the combination. Financial assistance may be needed during the first phase.

The other option is beginning with the secular job and only later taking on the ecclesiastical. Guy Kagey in Washington County, New York, and Bennington County, Vermont, first became known as a teacher and helper of slow learners in the two contiguous counties. He was already self-supporting. An ecclesiastical "auxiliary clergy" status came only later. The criterion in mind remains the same;

acknowledged character and authority in a community or area in a settled way before launching out into tentmaking.

Organizations

The tentmaker movement is not yet organized, but there are beginnings. In the Roman Catholic Church there is the Society of Priests for a Free Ministry,[9] with 1300 names on its lists. There is also the National Committee on the Permanent Diaconate. In the Episcopal Church, December, 1971, saw the organization of the Non-Stipendiary Training and Organization Program (Non-STOP) involving non-stipendiary priests and deacons, trainers of the same, diocesan Commissions on Ministry interested in this arena of action, active diocesan training programs, and interested sympathizers and resource people.

Settings

Tentmaking ministries offer a way to make a church which is too small for a full-time, resident pastor become viable and a credit to the Lord. Most people in the pew want as a pastor a man of their community, living with them and sharing their lives. Whether the tentmaker earns his living in that community or not, if he lives there the resident pastorate is furthered. Such is the case with the Methodist pastor of Easton, New York, who works in an educational job in Troy but resides in the manse in the lovely little hamlet on the upper Hudson River. Other churches may be too small to have the full-time services of a really professional specialist assistant. The problem was magnificently solved at Grace Church, Madison, Wisconsin, where in the 1950's Robert Gard presided over University of Wisconsin English classes, wrote childrens' books, and at the same time organized in the parish a fabulous series of programs, in which the Christian faith and the literary and plastic arts interacted.[10] This was a wonderful part-time ministry which bridged town and gown. A third setting for tentmaking ministries is many small "at-work churches," house-churches, or neighborhood-church units, serving people who would never darken the door of a normal church.

Warnings

One negative factor must be noted. The way forward is through a *first-class effort* in both seminary training and locally-prepared tentmakers. A host of diocesan seminaries and training programs have sprung up (in the Episcopal Church alone in such places as Los Angeles, Minnesota, Albany, Long Island, Michigan, and the Dakotas). Some of these do a first-class job. But some simply give a second-class preparation for the old way of ministry. On weekends and at night they train candidates who continue in secular positions, but with the idea that upon ordination, the new clergy will leave their secular employ behind. Thus there is no relationship between secular life and ecclesiastical ministry. Another experiment being tried is for seminary committees to make one of the criteria for admission the stipulation that a candidate must have another means by which to support himself. In many cases, this procedure begs the real question. If a man leaves behind a technical field, such as insurance or engineering, for three years, he will be rusty and incompetent in it upon ordination. Also, how is the secular to be related to the ecclesiastical creativity? A seminary must implement such requirements with career development help or ministerial supervision leading to meaningful combinations of the secular and ecclesiastical, or at least allowing a man to keep up secular skills while learning ecclesiastical ones.

An alternative approach to the usual type of graduate

seminary education is offered by Dr. John Fletcher's
Inter-Met in Washington, President Bill Webber's New York
Theological Seminary in New York City, and Dean Michael
Allen's Berkeley Divinity School at Yale in New Haven, in
which secular skills and ecclesiastical training may be
combined in actual secular settings for the practice of
ministry. Here, it seems to me, are models of the direction in
which to move for training tentmakers in an area where there
is no hard and fast line between the sacred and secular, the
profane and holy, the secular and ecclesiastical. The Action
Training Coalition of training institutes in the church can also
be helpful.[1] [1]

Another danger comes because of the present "clergy
surplus" in many denominations, such as the Episcopalians
and the United Church of Christ. The growing movement
into the tentmaking ministry seems at present to involve
mostly seminary-trained men. In a static situation, where new
work is not developed, this will limit the possibility of the
locally-chosen and trained type of minister, who in the long
run may prove the most effective because of his local base.

However, there is a growing number of unchurched
Americans, a growing need for new work, and a growing
number of tentmakers can afford to undertake the same
because they do not need church salaries and buildings in
order to perform ministry and evangelism. There may be
trouble in getting the ecclesiastical hierarchy to authorize
new work, but if the target of new ministry units is clearly
understood to be not someone else's sheep but the "I never
thought I'd be connected with the church!" type, then this
should be mitigated. If we are genuinely serious about the
evangelism of the unchurched, we can offer a multitude of
opportunity.

Another danger I foresee is the old school tie,

seminary/clubman syndrome. For some two to three centuries, the ordained ministry, at least in most main line denominations, has been associated with a certain class or status, one of the entrance marks into which is finishing a certain graduate level of higher education. In the face of rapid change and the ordained ministry being looked on by the general public as of relatively lower status than before, the reaction of some old style clergy (and there are many such around) is to draw back behind an armor plate composed of one part graduate school education as preparation for ordination, and one part full-time clerical gentility, treating non-graduate seminary men as second class clergy, and putting pressure against the training of locally raised up men who do not leave their home roots for at least a year (and preferably three to four) at a graduate school of religion. It is even reliably reported that such pressure by seminary trained clergy is causing the Hong Kong and Idaho diocesan training programs in the Anglican Church to cease the preparation of any locally raised up and trained men for the present.

The answer to this danger I see only in emphasizing the *calling* to the ordained ministry, and de-emphasizing the social status attached to the same. This is a realistic move in a day when the ordained ministry is a higher-risk, lower-status profession than before. And it also puts the emphasis on the *mission* of the clergy, not on their rights and status.

Summary

We have considered a problem: what looked like too many, too-small congregations, with all the attendant implications for lay and clerical ministry. We have seen a solution in the growing movement towards tentmaking ministry, which combines secular livelihood and ecclesiastical function. This makes smaller places viable, freeing energy and time and finances for mission. It also opens ways for specialized ministries and for small units which can minister to those who would not darken the door of a traditional church edifice. The last few decades have seen an incredible variety of types, sorts, and groups of self-supporting ministries, and we have tried to describe them in this chapter. The problem now is reorientation of the institutional church to approve the tentmaking ministry and to facilitate its expression as one of the instruments for beginning new work. In essence, the problem is motivating an institution worried about institutional survival to undertake a new venture in mission.

Footnotes

1. *The Non-Stipendiary Ministry: A Preliminary Report — Profile,* Strategic Research, Executive Council, New York, October, 1970; and *A New Approach to Ministry: The Non-Stipendiary Clergy,* Ministry Council, Episcopal Church Center, New York, October, 1971.
2. For a fuller discussion, see Boyd, Malcolm (Ed.), *The Underground Church,* New York, Sheed & Ward, 1968. Dr. Benignus recently moved to Inter-Met, Washington, D.C.
3. For these insights I am indebted to Joan B. Miller, whose "The Casework Ministry" is slated for publication by SPCK in London in 1972.
4. Allen, Roland, *Missionary Methods: St. Paul's or Ours?;* also *The Spontaneous Expansion of the Church;* and *The Ministry of the Spirit;* all published in paperback by Eerdmans, Grand Rapids, 1962.
5. I am indebted for the substance of this typology to John J. Lloyd, a student of Roland Allen's book and a distinguished returned missionary from Japan.
6. *Cf.* Lowery, James L., Jr., "Small Congregations and Their Clergy," monograph published in 1970 by the Association of Episcopal Clergy; available from 8 Newbury Street, Boston, Mass. 02116.
7. For further elucidation, see the 1971 documentation packet, "An Exploration into Worker Ministries," by Serge Hummon, United Church of Christ Board for Homeland Ministries, Division of Church Extension.
8. *Cf.* recommendations section, p. 10 *ff.,* of this author's 1970 monograph, "Small Congregation and Their Clergy" (see footnote 6 above).
9. See pp. 92 *ff.*

10. This example and many others came from the experience of Dr. H. Boone Porter. Dr. Porter gives a very interesting traveling seminar on "New Models of Ministry."

11. Addresses available from Urban Training Center for Christian Mission, 21 East Van Buren, Chicago, Illinois 60605.

CHAPTER SIX

Overeducated and Underemployed

Introduction

A final problem area this book intends to look at is what we might call the overeducated and underemployed state of many of the local clergy. The recession in the early 1970's has revealed many Ph.D.'s who were not hireable, because companies preferred master's and bachelor's degree holders at lower salary scales and expectations. With the clergy, the situation has been a bit different: many clergy, highly trained, skilled and motivated to work hard and long, but kept in positions of insufficient challenge, need, and workload. In the Episcopal Church, I would estimate that about one-half the clergy are overeducated and underemployed.

One of the basic causes of this situation seems to be *too many too-small local congregations* to use professional skills and men properly.[1] If over half of the local ministry units of a denomination serve 200 adult supporters or less on an annual budget of $20,000 or less, the result will be low compensation for the professional clergyman, lack of adequate secretarial, janitorial, and paraprofessional help, and not a great deal going on to keep the highly trained professional involved. The clergyman spends less time on counselling and teaching, which are highly skilled functions, because there just are not many persons in his flock to teach and counsel.

Another cause seems to be the *highly skilled and trained person* expected to be the average parish pastor in the normal main line Christian congregation. We expect of our pastors at least seven years of higher education, normally four at the college level and three in a professional school. We expect him to be conversant with theology at the graduate level, trained to some degree in the behavioral and managerial sciences, and able as a pastoral theologian to apply theology to the concrete practice of ministry on the local scene. How well this training has been or is being done is another question. The point, for our investigation, is that we are requiring the services, at the local level, of an expensively trained professional who has been acclimatized to an upper middle-class, professional-level style of life. Obviously, clergy do not become rich on the average compensation tendered them, but the fact is that in the too many too-small congregations, fifty per cent and more of the budget goes for the support of the clergyman. In my last pastoral charge, exactly one-half of the budgets of my two churches went for my stipend, allowances, and perquisites, which were minimal. In the parish I presently serve as a voluntary assistant, sixty-five per cent of the parish budget goes for the support of the rector. This is not to begrudge decent salaries for the clergy; they should be even higher. But it is to say that we may be demanding a more highly educated and trained professional man than the situation really requires. It simply does not take a high degree of organizational, administrative, and pastoral skill to head and serve a parish of 200 communicants in this day and age.

Examples

Let me cite two randomly chosen cases, one northern and one southern. The first comes out of the experiences of a devoted couple who are active communicants of a prosperous, large congregation in the north shore suburbs of Chicago. Initially because of a family funeral and later in the course of vacation travels, they made the acquaintance of a very personable and intelligent priest in Nebraska. They were surprised to find such an educated and skillful man serving a small congregation after twenty-seven years in the ordained ministry, not because he wished a specialized ministry of this kind, but because this was all that was offered him. In fact, he told them, it had taken him twenty years to get to the point that he had only one congregation to serve. Their worry was how deadening and frustrating it must be for him to serve in a position of little intellectual, organizational, and pastoral challenge.

I tried to explain to them how common this situation was, and to intimate that one should be grateful that fine, talented men will stay at such low-level service. However, there is a valid distinction between the giving of one's life to the Lord wherever he may call, and the subsequent training of such a person for a professional level task, only to ship him off to spend his life in a setting not requiring professional talents.

A second case is that of the early ministry of a young pastor named Hume Reeves, Jr., a "parsonage kid" who certainly knew what he was getting into in the pastorate. Several years out of seminary he found himself still assigned to a small mission church and helping out as a part-time assistant in a larger parish nearby. There were so few people and so little work that the only way this highly motivated and spiritual professional was able to keep his sanity was to go fishing three days a week! He respected the persons he served and knew their thoughts must be, "How long will we be keeping him? When will he get fed up, and whom will they bring in next and for how long?" He frantically looked for community and judicatory work to do, both to keep himself busy and to keep his hand in the work he was trained for.

Options

Here is the plight of many overeducated and underemployed clergy in modern American main line denominations. And it is not only a Protestant phenomenon. A look at a monograph such as Watzky's "Saturday Night and Sunday"[2] shows that similar conditions are common in the Roman Catholic Church, in terms of work if not in terms of parish size. A very busy weekend in most parishes is followed by a quiet midweek, with either a great deal of time off taken, or else various ecclesiastical activities or community jobs voluntarily undertaken to fill the time. Choosing additional activities confronts the underemployed clergyman with at least seven options.

A first option, chosen by many pastors, is to keep themselves *busy-busy* by spending time on activities which could perfectly well be done, in fact preferably should be done, by well qualified lay persons in the congregation. While this keeps the pastor busy, it stifles lay initiative, and it represents a lowering of the activity level of the professional clergyman. Examples of this sort of lowering are keeping accounts, banking the collections, supervising bingo and fairs, etc.

A second choice made by clergy in this situation is the *lazy-lazy* option. These clergy are realistic enough to see there is just not much work to be done. They do that amount and precious little else. They slide back into living a third of a life and talk about how much work those few duties they do have constitute. One hears them complain about how hard it is to get through one popular ecclesiastical weekly. They never read solid theological tomes. And the public in general, seeing how little they do and the lazy character thereby engendered, have an image of the pastorate as a way of life for the incompetent.

The third option is to *take to the bottle or to sleep around town.* As one whose office space is in an alcoholism institute whose director is a charter member of the Recovered Alcoholic Clergy Association, I see the frequency of the former; as a busy counsellor of clergy in crisis, I know the increasing number of the latter. In my opinion, these third-option types are superior to the "lazy-lazies." At least they take some action in their situation, no matter how perverted.

A fourth choice is to opt for what we might call "*the classic sinecure.*" This is an option hoary with tradition, especially in my own Anglican heritage. One accepts the fact that the basic pastoral charge will require a minimum of work, does that faithfully, and then spends the remainder of the time at some completely unrelated hobby pursued as an amateur. One has to recall how talented some of this amateurism has been and how much of the findings of eighteenth and nineteenth century philosophy, biology, philology, and economics, from Berkeley to Malthus, came out of rectories and vicarages. And I see parsonages nowadays where for mental survival the pastor spends great time and effort in such pursuits as cabinet making and shell collecting.

The fifth option is *moving to tentmaking status*[3] , especially when the small amount of pastoral work yields a salary insufficient to eat on.

The figures are not yet clear, but the supposition, conservatively arrived at, in such a main line denomination as the Episcopal Church, is that fifteen to twenty per cent of the clergy now receive the majority of their income from secular sources.

An interesting example is an insurance man turned Anglican priest who has returned to the insurance business in Connecticut. Here is his tale, in the words of an interviewer:

One insurance man said he had left selling insurance in his thirties because he felt there was need of his services in the ministry. He found at fifty that the church was not crying for his talents, and that although he felt he had done a good journeyman job of being a parish priest, there was no significant career development now opening up before him in this field, and possible income was not adequate for his needs.

... The church's feeling was that he would be doing a real service by getting himself out of the way as competition for the more substantial parishes, or embarrassing the church by staying in a position it knew was not challenging enough for him. So, being free from any sense of duty to stay in the parochial field, he went back to insurance.

He said that the ways in which he had grown during his pastorate had magnified his capacity to sell insurance, and he felt he was now doing as well as he would have learned to do by this time if he had stayed in insurance...

He had, however, lost the building up of commissions coming in from renewals, but he expected to make this up in even larger proportions. He worked with a clear conscience because when his church called him he had answered the call, and now was free to go back to his first vocation. The only thing was he would like now to be free to go back to his old layman's kind of service (on church boards, etc.) but priests are suspicious of other priests in layman's roles and you have to tread lightly.[4]

A sixth option is that of community and missionary work. Its necessary presupposition is that the support of the clergyman is sufficient financially so that he is free to do other things with little thought of remuneration. The best current description of this approach is to be found in James D. Glasse's *Putting It Together in the Parish.*[5] Glasse sees the local ministry situation of many pastors as having a unique amount of freedom because "paying the rent," as he calls it, takes only a minor portion of the time. The pastor is expected to provide a well prepared worship experience on Sunday and special days, some decent nurture experiences for various ages (especially the young), to take pastoral care of his flock, and to provide a sufficient amount of organizational and administrative coordination to allow all this to go on. The total time for these activities just does not take up the whole week. They are "the rent" which allows the pastor the rest of the time free. He may then use the time for missionary activity or for work in the community. The congregation looks upon such work as "the rector's wild ideas," or "the pastor's personal interests," humors him in it, and freely allows it to go on, once the basic chores are done. Ironically it is usually this special work for which the pastor is remembered and which makes a lasting contribution.

A seventh option is *consultative work.* The pastor finds himself especially competent in one area, develops this competence into a specialty in which he has special accreditation and acknowledged expertise, and spends time helping others in that field. The consultation is carried on in other parish or community situations than his own, for the pastor "is not without honor save in his own country!" He may or may not receive outside remuneration for the service. Thus, for years the rector of St. Thomas's Episcopal Church, North Syracuse, New York, was the youth education expert and consultant for the Diocese of Central New York; and the pastor of Houghton, Michigan, the educational consultant in town and country ministry for the (North-Midwest) Fifth Province of the Episcopal Church. Consultation more outside one's local purview would be represented by the Parish Associates of Project Test Pattern (headquarters in Washington, D.C.), who come out of their own parishes in teams of two to do organizational development work in other congregations and agencies.

Similarities to Other Occupations

We have described a situation: the clergy being overeducated and underemployed. We have seen some of its causes and some of its results. But it is only fair to try to put it into a larger context, and to add that in many respects this situation is not unique to the pastorate.

For example, the early-1970 teachers' glut resembles it in some respects. Due to the retrenchment in National Aeronautical and Space Agency activities and reduced funding by government and other agencies, to universities, on the one hand, and the great numbers of teachers at all levels coming out of teachers' colleges across the land, on the other, there has been a nationwide surplus of teachers, and many Ph.D.'s have found themselves teaching secondary subjects in schools. What seems to be unusual about the clergy situation is the lack of sufficient local ministry situations large enough or varied enough to require truly professional level talent.

A previous chapter of this book has gone into the subject of tentmaking ministries as an option for the overeducated and underemployed clergyman. But there has been little consideration yet of clergy as consultants, of the parson as "wise old owl." It is to this increasing practice of clergy, while in their parishes, serving also as specialized consultants externally, that we now turn.

Footnotes

1. See Chapter IV of this book.
2. James Watzke, Department of Social Relations, 1967-68, Harvard University.
3. See Chapter V.
4. He was interviewed by the Rev. Jervis Zimmerman at a conference for 20-odd non-stipendiary non-parochial clergymen in that judicatory, held June 24, 1972 at Wykeham Rise School, Washington, Conn. My citations come from the Rev. John Knoble, tentmaker priest and pastor of the diocese, who is also a professional teacher and feature writer for the New Haven *Register*.
5. Abingdon, Nashville, 1972.

CHAPTER SEVEN

Owls

More and more clergy are to be found developing consultation and spending a part of their time serving as consultants outside their own parish. This work is done in other parishes, in church-related or community-related settings, or through consultative relationships of a completely secular character. It is my contention that this ought to be encouraged. The clergyman can be used several parishes distant from his home, and he may use consultants from several parishes away in his own setting. What results makes not only for better use of the human resources of the church, but it also furthers an interdependent, collaborative style of ministry which is well suited to our time. And it engages the the many talents of the clergyman at a suitable level.

A Plethora of Skills and Talents

For generations the parish pastor of priest has been a jack-of-all-trades, a possessor of many skills. In the traditional setting of one parson and a small congregation serving a neighborhood or village, the need was for a clergyman with a variety of talents, from public speaking to healing, from moral theology to counselling at law, from administering the sacraments to public welfare work, from preaching to schoolmastering. In a day when Thomas Jefferson could keep in touch with all areas of learning from his Monticello hilltop, the parson could be a jack-of-all-trades from the colonial rectory. Not yet had the law and medicine and social work emerged as separate professions. The parson was usually the best educated man of the community, more in touch with the knowledge needed for professional practice than anyone else around.

We have already described the process which has removed much professional and skilled practice from the parsonage to other offices in the town and metropolis.[1] We have mentioned the consequent decline in the status of the clergyman. Yet there remains in the practice of ministry, as carried out by the experienced pastor, a wide array of skills.

My own perception is that it is the particular combination of ministry skills and experience taken together as a functional unity of practical ministry which constitutes the minister as a professional.[2] Special emphasis on and training in certain of these skills can qualify the parson as a consultant, able to help others in his particular area of expertise. For some clergy this may be administration, for others the planning process, for some youth work, for some education and training, for some social action, for some community organization, for some communications, for others retreats or prayer. The list could stretch on. Let me cite but one example, that of a Maryknoll priest on mission in the Philippines whom we shall call Larry Braun. Larry administered three to five churches which in turn served about forty evangelistic stations. He found that the best persons in the mountain villages of his area, in terms both of status in the community and time available for catechetics and missioning, were grandmothers. These he commissioned as resident, front-line lay evangelists, to supplement the itinerant ministry of ordained missionaries such as himself, who could then do their thing on hilltops, surrounded by

crowds from a large area. The results were a spectacular
increase in baptisms, while at the same time the requirements
and standards for becoming a Christian were raised. Upon
returning to this country to take on other work, Larry went
for professional career development consultancy. He soon
learned that his skills and experience in the Philippines
showed him to be a first-class salesman and sales director, an
eminent planner, strategist, and tactician, a resourceful
manager of people and administrator of sub-units of a
regional organization. While Braun's tale may be more
spectacular than the average, it is not so far out of line with
what the ordinary pastor in the parish could claim. It is my
contention, as a professional career and ministry development consultant, that in the normal setting of the parish, the
pastor who has survived and been able to accomplish any real
in-depth ministry to the Christian community and beyond,
has done so because he has had significant administrative,
organizational, diplomatic, and sales skills.

I have seen skill development proceed by two paths. One
is taking a skill acquired in secular life and applying it to the
ordained ministry. Such is the case with Father Robert Field,
who uses his skill and experience as a combat medic from
World War II to be a member and chaplain of the rescue
squad or fire department, wherever he is resident as parish
priest.[3] Another example is the Reverend Walter Lardner of
Hudson Falls, New York, who uses his insurance background
to check out the policies of all Episcopal churches in his
nineteen-county diocese and serves as an unpaid consultant
to parishes both in his own and neighboring dioceses.

The other path is that of recognizing a need, getting the
necessary skills and training for dealing with it, and then
becoming a helper or consultant in the chosen area. Such is
the Reverend David DeVore, who found a community need

for work with homeless and adolescents, got the training and accreditation, and was catalyst in the organization of a residential treatment institution for troubled, emotionally disturbed boys in Madison, Wisconsin. He is now also a consultant to others in the field.[4]

Society, Knowledge-Economy, and the Church

The Middle Ages were characterized by slow movement and stability. There may have been violence, disease, and shortness of life incomprehensible to a modern American, but there still was continuity. Modern, post-industrial America, however, is characterized by transience and acceleration, says Toffler.[5] Especially has knowledge accelerated. Luckily, at the same time the ability to make decisions using an immense amount of data has been enhanced by the use of the computer. Computer programming can control a mushrooming amount of knowledge and use it to help a man make more decisions and affect more things than he was ever able to do before.

John Kenneth Galbraith identifies three key factors in modern economics: technology (or knowledge), capital, and skilled management capable of using the knowledge and capital for problem-solving, planning, producing, and profit.[6]

But the clincher on the subject of modern society, of which the church is a part, is provided by management consultant and teacher Peter F. Drucker.[7] He sees our world as having moved from an economy dominated by the production of goods to an economy with the majority of the gross national product generated by services, and about to move into a "knowledge-economy," where the key persons will be those who can relate knowledge-resources to ways of using them in an organization. Such a person is the modern consultant!

Drucker also sees the modern society as a society increasingly composed of organizations. Business, educational, voluntary, and religious organizations are proliferating and growing increasingly interdependent. Not only are business organizations growing in number and in scope; the growth of voluntary associations and non-profit associations is an increasingly powerful force economically.[8] Here new coordinating structures, from associations of organizations to coordinating councils of metropolitan community services, are needed. In the religious field, a wide variety of denominational, interchurch, and independent organizations and agencies have joined the local congregation and denominational judicatories on the ecclesiastical bench.[9] A case in point would be the mushrooming in the last fifty years of religious agencies that are now listed in *The Official Catholic Directory* (P.J. Kenedy) and the growing number of sub-agencies coordinated by the National Council of Catholic Bishops and the National Catholic Conference. What is increasingly needed is the person skilled in the resource areas these organizations cover in interfacing these organizations with each other, and trained in applied social psychology and sociology. Such again is the description of the background of many modern consultants.

The church has begun to recognize and to use consultant skills. Let me list three examples from my own experience as an Episcopalian doing a certain amount of national and interdenominational work.

The Joint Commission on Structure of the General Convention, under the chairmanship of Bishop John Craine of Indianapolis, has been working to restructure the national Episcopal administrative and legislative structure, as well as to develop criteria for a viable diocese. For the work on legislative structure and the instrumentalities of General

Convention between its triennial meetings, it engaged the services of Booz, Allen and Hamilton, management consultants, who listened, gathered data, made recommendations, and presented them to the Joint Commission. Some of the recommendations, such as a full-time secretary of convention, are now in effect.

Another example was the hiring of a consultant to aid the Executive Council in the reduction of its professional staff during the ecclesiastical financial crisis of the early 1970's. The consultant helped set up a well-defined process for laying off staff, helping them to find other positions, and giving them a bonus for leaving any month *before* the actual date of severance. Still another example was the use of Information Sciences, Inc., by several denominations under a Rockefeller Brothers Fund grant to research the guidelines for what became known as the Church Manpower System, and some years later to aid the Episcopalians, Lutheran Church in America, and American Baptist Convention in setting up computerized personnel-listing systems.

A final example would be the use of outside "vacancy" consultants by many parishes between pastors, in order to aid them through the "grief work" over their former pastors, assess the point at which they now stood, set some realistic goals for years ahead, and in that light plan the resources, equipment, and personnel needed. Only then would they write a position description which would the basic tool used in the search for a new pastor.

Definitions and Models

Perhaps it would be well to backtrack at this point in order to come up with definitions of an organization, and of a consultant.

An organization is defined as a system coordinating the

different actions of individual contributors and units in order to carry out planned transactions with the environment.[10] In applying this to religious and voluntary systems, one must decide which is the basic building block to be regarded as the "system" — the denomination, the diocese or judicatory, or the individual local congregation.For practical, day-to-day purposes involving most pastors, the local parish may be chosen as the system or organization.

A healthy organization may be defined as one that efficiently and humanely achieves its goals in a changing environment.

A consultant is "a professional person who enters into mutually satisfactory agreements with an organization or subsystem of that organization: 1) to examine the problems of the organization, 2) to determine the objectives, goals and style of the organization, 3) to identify the degree to which persons, programs and policies of the organization are fulfilling the objectives thereof, and 4) to develop ways which might help movement towards better organizational performance."[11] The essence of the consultant relationship is that help is never really help unless it is perceived as helpful by the recipient, regardless of the helper's good intentions. And a corollary is that the consultant's responsibility is not to do work for the client organization, but to help the client see the situation fully and realistically, consider alternatives, make decisions, find and use appropriate resources, and make the most of potential abilities.[12] He or she may be an external consultant, one from outside the organization; or an in-house consultant, one whose job is within the organization but who contracts to deal on a non-stipendiary basis with another part of the organization.

There are three models of consultation.[13] The first is the *purchase model,* often called the rational-bureaucratic model.

Here the client defines the need and buys a prognosis, analysis, and proposed solution from the consultant. An example would be the National Joint Commission on Structure of the Episcopal Church buying the services of Booz, Allen and Hamilton, to recommend a new legislative structure.

A second model of consultation might be called the *doctor-patient model,* in which the consultant and client together define the need but the consultant gives the prognosis and recommended solution, which is then accepted or rejected by the client. An example of this type of consultation was the original contract between several denominations and Information Science, Inc. to deal with a manpower problem, which resulted in a recommendation acceptable to only one of the client denominations, the American Baptist Convention.

The third (and to this biased observer the preferable) mode of consultancy is called *process consultation.*[14] Here there must be mutual agreement between consultant and client at every stage of the consultation. The opposite side of the coin is that all through the process the client is learning how to diagnose his own problems. Thus he gains new skills, many of which he may retain. It is truly an enabling experience for him and his organization. The consultant and the client are both in on the diagnosis and decision-making, so that what transpires is not an acceptance or rejection of a specific proposal, but rather a decision in which all parties have shared. An example of this is the second contract between Information Sciences, Inc., and the American Baptist Convention, Episcopal Church, and Lutheran Church in America task forces, which together asked questions about the kinds of information needed, made decisions, and set up what was called personnel support services in the American

Baptist Convention, personnel development in the Lutheran
Church in America and the Clergy Deployment Office
personnel listing service in the Episcopal Church.

We have noted how the church and other institutions have
begun to make use of consultants. Before considering
additional examples, there remain three things to say.

The first is that consultants normally bring two kinds of
resources: a knowledge of what makes an organization
healthy or keeps it that way, and a background in the
content area with which the organization is dealing.[1][5] When
I undertake a contract with a judicatory personnel
committee, for example, I come both as a person with skills
in helping that committee deal fruitfully with its
constituency, but also with some expertise in the field of
clergy career development. In a sense this is wearing two hats.
But this is all right so long as it is clear that my commitment
is to the health of the organization and the individuals
involved, not to any specific new program. The task-orienta-
tion is the responsibility of the client committee. The
consultant's orientation is to organizational health that will
enable those tasks to be efficiently and humanely performed.
By the same token, financial consultants brought into an
undercapitalized company have both a health-and-growth
process orientation, and a financial competence. But they do
not push a decision for the purpose of seeing that it is carried
out. They rather involve themselves and the client company
in a process which results in the company seeing specific
needs and choosing specific ways of raising capital. We are
ultimately talking about a collaborative and trusting
interrelationship.

The second opinion I have to offer is that certain kinds of
groups seem to be more open to using consultants, and more
skilled in making profitable use of them, than others. Many

church bodies use consultants badly. Either they explain themselves badly and do not share with consultants because they want to hear themselves talk, or they dump the whole burden and responsibility on the consultants. Thus, some consultants will have nothing to do with church work. However, two kinds of groups stand out as exceptions. Both take for granted a situation of rapid change, and this may explain their ability to work with consultants, who are in a sense professional change agents. The two groups are special ministries/special agencies and the professional clergy associations. On the whole, regular church judicatories and congregations do not use consultants well, although there are splendid exceptions. I think especially of the flexibility of the North Conway Institute, a church-connected national agency dealing with the field of alcohol and drug abuse, which has moved vigorously and flexibly in the last decade, helped by the consultative skills of Consultation/Search, Inc., of Cambridge, Massachusetts, changing from essentially a programming organization to a more consultative/catalyst one. I think also of the fruitful growth and change in the character of the Academy of Parish Clergy, soon after engaging the services of Byrd & Jones of Minneapolis. Also of St. Peter's Lutheran Church in New York City, which is making very fruitful use of Consultation/Search to define its mission and the future use of its fabric and resources in a new way.

The third point is that the practice of developing usable (and salable!) consultant skills is a sage thing in a time of declining financial support for the ecclesiastical institution, with little decline as yet in the number of persons graduating from seminary and seeking ordination. The clergy surplus means that a secular financial base will be necessary for a large percentage of future clergy by the end of this decade.

There is still the need for many more clergy to do the mission of Christ in areas yet untouched. But they cannot expect to be paid. Thus the "moonlighting" character of some consultant work can be a base from which to move into the tentmaking or non-stipendiary kind of ministry described in an earlier chapter.

In-House Consultants

We now turn to a description of consultant work and relationships, and we begin with those fully within the institutional church. The first type of consultant is the person employed at the judicatory or national level who has been trained in a variety of consultant skills and who contracts to use some of them on an individual agreement basis with other units of his judicatory or with congregations or special ministries in his ecclesiastical region. The great-granddaddy of this type is the "educational consultant" on the staff of so many different judicatories, from an archdiocesan Confraternity of Christian Doctrine to a conference board of education. For a generation or two now, the presence and use of this sort of consultant has become well established. Out of it has grown the kind of consultant who serves a region, has an array of skills, and contracts to use some of them in each individual situation on an *ad hoc* basis. Let me cite three current examples in my own denomination. The first is Bill Yon, program director of the Episcopal Diocese of Alabama, and executive secretary of the Association for Religion and the Applied Behavioral Sciences. He is accredited in the areas of sensitivity training, program design and development, Christian education, and organizational development, both as a consultant to groups and organizations and as a trainer of persons in skills in these areas. He works part time in each area, on an individual agreement basis, as a consultant. Second is James Anderson, assistant for parish development to the Episcopal bishop of Washington, who works in the areas of planning, vacancy consultation, organizational development, and training. He too spends part of his time in each area, mostly on an individual agreement basis. Third is John C. Harris, who serves a Joint Commission on Clergy Development of the Episcopal Dioceses of Washington and Maryland. His bag of tricks is in the area of enabling individual clergy from selection through retirement, rather than enabling congregations and organizations, as in the case of Anderson.

My inference from a description of these three is that much of what they do is similar to the work of a parish priest, with some highly developed skills utilized part time as a consultant in a chosen field. The Reverend John Conn, rector of the Episcopal Church in Hopkinton, Massachusetts, is also the diocesan coordinator/consultant for clergy continuing education. A percentage of his time, agreed upon by both parish and diocese, is given to the consultancy. The Reverend Fordyce Eastburn, while still a hospital chaplain in the California (San Francisco Bay) Episcopal Diocese, gave a stated portion of his time as a placement consultant for the diocese. Still other examples are the diocesan teams of organizational consultants to parishes and special ministries/agencies trained and coordinated by the Episcopal Dioceses of Maryland and North Carolina, the Baltimore Conference of the United Methodist Church, and the Central Atlantic Conference of the United Church of Christ. Most of these men are parish pastors and directors of religious education, who have agreements with their congregations and judicatories to give a certain amount of their time to consultancy with clients on an individual agreement basis.

External Consultants

Perhaps the majority of consultancy is done by external or outside consultants. These have no prior pecuniary relationship to the system or subsystem with which they have consultant relationships. They come from one congregation to another congregation. Or they come from an outside network to a special ministry. Or they operate out of a consultative agency or firm. The internal consultant has the insider's advantage of being already partly trusted by the clients and having considerable knowledge of the norms and cultures he deals with. The disadvantage of being an internal consultant is that his being on the payroll may influence him against suggesting radical alternatives, such as those that might change or do away with his job! The advantage of the external consultant is his objectivity and ability to pursue a full range of alternatives, and his bringing a fresh perspective and view into play. The disadvantage of the external consultant is that he is seen as a foreign expert and has to establish his credibility and trustworthiness in the organization he is to help.

In any case, a large number and variety of persons are undertaking work as external consultants in ecclesiastical, voluntary, and non-profit settings.

First, there are the old-line management consultant firms already mentioned. Booz, Allen and Hamilton worked with the Joint Commission on Structure of the Episcopal Church. Harbridge House worked with three New England dioceses of the Episcopal Church on a manpower management survey.[16]

Next come the research, training, and organizational development consultancy firms which were formed by former parish priests or judicatory and national staff persons to be a permanent base for utilizing their consultant skills, either full time or part time. Such are Byrd & Jones of

Minneapolis, Ecumenical Consultants, Inc., of Oradell, New Jersey and Sebastopol, California, and Peabody Organizational Development, Inc., of New York.[17] Richard Byrd and David Jones come from a background that includes the parish ministry as education and training in the Episcopal Church on the national level. Seeing the financial crunch of the early '70's about to hit the church and foreseeing a drastic cut in the number of professional staff employed, further recognizing that research, development, and training people are always the first to go, they set up their own consulting and training firm. They help voluntary and profit-making organizations, parishes, and businessses all over the country. Ecumenical Consultants, Inc. grew out of the unit of field study, subsequently the Division of Strategic Research Services in the Episcopal Church, which produced a series of landmark studies on the clergy and had gathered data for more reports, when it was abolished in the mass firings of 1970 and 1971. David Covell and John McCarty subsequently formed E.C.I. and continue to do substantially the same work, giving about one-half time to this and the other half to work as pastors of small parishes in the Atlantic and Pacific areas respectively. George Peabody was first a parish priest in Maryland with special competence in education and training, and then a pioneer in the development of parish life laboratories, the application of the behavioral sciences to program design in voluntary and religious systems, and organizational work in various settings. He now does consultancy work from a New York City base and serves on the staff of the noted career and organizational development program run every year by the Berkeley Center for Human Interaction in California.

Two other consultant organizations worth noting are Consultation/Search, Inc., of Cambridge, Massachusetts, and the Ecumenical Career Counselling Service of Melrose, Massachusetts, C/S Inc. does management consultancy, executive search, and curriculum training and design for churches, judicatories, agencies, institutions, and businesses. The owners are Henry Sherrill, Jones Shannon, and John Soleau, three clergymen with backgrounds in the parish pastorate, investment counselling, college work, communications, administration, and the Harvard Business School. Ecumenical Career Counselling Service is the brainchild of the Reverend Alfred Zadig and does career development consultancy. Zadig's background is in the parish priesthood, community organization, Office of Economic Opportunity work, and career transition counselling with the national Bearings for Re-establishment network. It is worth noting at this point that some consultants are incorporated as profit-making organizations and others as non-profit agencies. Consultation/Search, Inc., and Peabody Organizational Development follow the for-profit route, whose legal status is relatively easy to obtain, while the others, in order to qualify for tax-free non-profit status, must go through a longer and more complicated process.

Another type of external consultant is the freelancer, skilled, accredited, and experienced, but operating on his own, legally and functionally. Two examples are the Reverend John Whiston of Capitola, California, who did educational consultancy with such entities as the Episcopal Diocese of San Joaquin, and the Reverend Edgar Lockwood of Washington, D.C., who is a consultant to mutual funds, corporations, and church funds on the social implications of investment, as well as editor of a newsletter called "The Responsible Investor."

The most interesting development in the way of consultancy, it seems to me, is the consultant network, with a nucleus of one or two part-time or full-time coordinators, surrounded by a web of consultant/trainers who are mostly practicing parish pastors. Examples are SALT Associates, Project Test Pattern, the National Training Labs, and the Center for A Voluntary Society. This is a phenomenon which seems both to use talented men effectively and at the same time to make parishes, ministries, agencies, and organizations much more effective in the fulfillment of their tasks and missionary goals.

I arbitrarily choose Project Test Pattern and its network as an example of highly skilled, otherwise underemployed clergy acting as part-time, experienced, and accredited consultants through a network. I do this for several reasons. One is that I have been personally acquainted with it almost since its very inception. Another is that its particular focus is bringing consultant teams of two to four persons from a brace of parishes to other parishes. Finally, its model from the beginning has contained a communications and research component for drawing lessons from the consultant process which would be valuable to the church at large. The Reverend Loren Mead is director of P.T.P., and Ms. Elisa DesPortes, research associate.[18] While much of the effort has been concentrated of necessity within the Episcopal Church. the project has had a strong ecumenical thrust.

The beginning of Project Test Pattern was within the National Advisory Commission on Evangelism of the Episcopal Church. Both Bishop Robert R. Brown (now retired) of Arkansas and the Right Reverend John E. Hines, Presiding Bishop, have been most helpful. The commission was established in its present form in 1967. Upon Bishop Brown's retirement, the Right Reverend Lloyd Gressle, now Episcopal Bishop of Bethlehem, Pennsylvania, became chairman. Project Test Pattern is the experimental program in parish renewal sponsored by this commission.

The background of P.T.P. is an understanding that one of the best instruments for evangelism is in the parish system of local congregations. There is no substitute for a local expression of the rhythm of mission and nurture as a force for evangelism. Other ministries may be more effective in certain areas, and regional and national church structures are necessary in the interdependent nature of modern society, but the parish system of local congregations is still potent in the fight against sin, negligence, and ignorance.

Historically there have been several models of local renewal. The first is the revival, from Wesley to Parish Life Weekends, from Sankey and Moody to Faith At Work. This way seems to have appealed to more conservative congregations and denominations, and to have had a limited impact on more liberal and more sacramental congregations, with some sterling exceptions. A second model has been clustering, or a grouping of local congregations bound together for common programs. Many things have been accomplished in this way. The United Presbyterian Church in the United States of America and the United Church of Christ officially encourage the practice, and a considerable fund of information is published and available about clusters. But this model seems to have less ability to weather changes of circumstances and leadership than do individual congregations. A third approach to evangelistic renewal is called leadership development (management development in the secular sphere). A major emphasis in denominations and in their educational institutions since World War II has thus been in ongoing training for clergy and others in academic areas, ministerial skills, and human relations. But time and time again the result is "hotted up" leadership returning to unprepared congregations and more frustration and unhealthiness than before. What is needed is an approach which does not allow a gap to grow between pastors and laity, of which Jeffrey Hadden writes.[19]

The model encouraged by Project Test Pattern is that of *parish development*. This approach to evangelism presupposes that the resources for a congregation are already within the congregation, and that the task is to unleash them and put them to work. The goal is to build the congregation into teams that can solve their own problems. A way to do this is by the in-parish intervention of skilled teams (two to four) of external consultants who bring objectivity, analytical skills, and resources for team building and conflict management, along with other specialized training.

Against this background, Project Test Pattern set to work in 1969 to accomplish three things:

1. Raise up a network of consultant/trainers, and a network of congregations which would be willing to be studied as well as to use the services of the consultants.

2. Learn from practice and experience if this model would make congregations more healthy and effective for evangelism and draw other lessons about the consultation process.

3. Communicate its research and findings to the church as a whole.

By the beginning of 1970 there was a network of six parishes on the East Coast, six parishes on the West, and thirty-two consultants in fourteen teams of two and one team of four. By the end of 1970, an ongoing relationship was formed with the Mid-Atlantic Training Committee, the Center for a Voluntary Society, and the National Training

Laboratories Institute. Case histories, an intervention handbook, and other materials were beginning to be written.

At this writing, P.T.P. has reached a cutoff point after recruiting additional parishes and consultants. No more regular parish consultants are being taken on, and no more consultants trained. The time between Spring, 1972, and the end of 1973 is being spent on three tasks: 1) concentrating on about two dozen vacancy consultations (where the parish is between pastors) in order to focus on a short crisis period when many places are open to using consultancy, and to draw conclusions from this; 2) publishing results and communicating them to the ecumenical church; and 3) closing up shop in a disciplined way that will leave a going network for consultation.

Lessons

Three lessons learned from the controlled and disciplined experimentation in parish renewal carried on by Project Test Pattern are especially applicable to the subject at hand.

The first is that the use of outside consultant intervention in the parish is now a proved method of getting results. It is a tested method of refocusing a congregation on its ministry and mission tasks and making the parish a more vital organization for carrying out these tasks. The method works in small and large congregations, in all geographical areas and social settings, and in more and less sacramentally-oriented contexts. What is required is a willingness to make a financial and mental commitment, to be open to change, to identify concrete goals and pursue them, to listen and dialogue, and to work through things, making decisions and efforts oneself, instead of dumping the whole load on outside experts.

The second lesson is that parish priests/pastors with proper training and experience, make very good consultants to other congregations. Most of the P.T.P-trained network is of such persons, giving a certain amount of time per month to consultancy work on an individual-contract basis, and having agreements with their home parishes that allow such work. Their home parishes are pleased to discover their pastors becoming more skillful. Client parishes are pleased with the consultant help. And this researcher is pleased with the way it puts to use in a fulfilling way many untapped skills of parish pastors.

A third lesson is the network concept, an instrument that fits in nicely with the knowledge economy mentioned earlier in this chapter. One of my board members is a cultural anthropologist whose main field of study is American Indians in white America.[20] But she receives information, suggestions, reactions, and criticisms which are helpful from a network of anthropologists, people in other behavioral disciplines, church agencies, graduate schools of education, Indian tribes, government agencies and community organizations, all of which overlap at least slightly. By the same token, there is a support system for consultants in the network of fellow consultants, Project Test Pattern, consultants in allied fields, the Association for Religion and the Applied Behavioral Sciences, the Center for a Voluntary Society, the National Training Laboratories Institute, the Mid-Atlantic Training Committee, and renewalist agencies of many types.

Criteria

One final area of concern must be mentioned. How does a person, an agency, or a congregation go about finding a trustworthy and competent consultant? Those who have had some experience with the encounter movement are understandably leery of some "practitioners" and "consultants." For these are new fields, with the persons active in them running the gamut from shysters to highly professional men and women. I offer three criteria for choosing consultants.

The first criterion is accreditation in the *content* area by the appropriate body. If it is social service consultancy, is the person a member of the American Council on Social Work? If it is architectural consultancy, is he a member of the American Institute of Architects? If psychological consultancy, what are his degrees, and is he a member of the American Psychological Association or some other reputable organization in the field? In my own work I am prepared to show that my abilities in ministry studies are recognized by the ecumenical Academy of Parish Clergy and the denominational clergy association movement, that my expertise in career development consultancy is certified by Human Resource Developers, Inc., who licensed me and who are themselves accredited by the International Association of Executive Consultants.

The second criterion is forming a judgment about a consultant is his accreditation in the *process* area of applying content to situations. Training or accreditation by such respected bodies as the Association for Religion and the Applied Behavioral Sciences, the National Training Laboratories Institute, *etc.* is an indication or professional competence here.

The third criterion is the most important. It is the *recommendation* of people who have used the consultants under consideration, assuming that the consultation relationship is finished. Asking a person's opinion of a consultant's ability in the early stages of the consultative relationship may be a bad move, because much of the helpfulness that a consultant can bring to an organization may depend upon helping that agency become "unstuck" and open to new ways of doing things at an early stage in the arrangements — a procedure which at that point may produce anxiety and temporary confusion.

Conclusion

We have examined several models of consultancy and chosen the "process consultation" approach as particularly effective in enabling churches and organizations to reset their sights and make decisions and implement them themselves. We have also seen that this self-determination with outside help principle can be a way to make local congregations more fit for evangelism. We have noted, in addition, growing networks of clergy who act as part-time consultants.

This process of consultation makes use of many parish pastors who would otherwise be overeducated and underemployed, who are now instead fulfilled in ministry, being most of the time about the work of the local pastorate, and part of the time in teams of external consultants, helping other congregations come alive. Here is a marvelous mushrooming movement in which the Holy Spirit is at work, which makes more creative ministry and furthers the Good News. Making more use of "owls" — experienced consultants — means good news to clergymen and to parishes.

Footnotes

1. *Cf.* Chapter I, "Introduction."
2. Section 3, "The Clergy as Professional, in monograph The Clergy, The Professional, and Preparation for Ordained Ministry," by James L. Lowery, Jr. in *St. Luke's Journal,* Sewanee, Tenn., Vol XIV, No. 4, Sept. 1971, and Vol. XV, No. 1, Jan. 1972, wherein much is borrowed from Dr. Seward Hiltner.
3. Now at an Episcopal Church in Ballston Spa, New York.
4. *Nashotah Review,* Vol. 12, No. 1, Fall 1971.
5. Toffler, Alvin, *Future Shock,* New York, Random House, 1970.

6. See especially Galbraith, J.K., *The Modern Industrial State,* Boston, Houghton Mifflin, 1967.

7. *Cf. The Age of Discontinuity; Guidelines to our Changing Society,* Peter F. Drucker, New York, Harper and Row, 1968 and 1969.

8. *Cf. Giving USA 1970,* American Association of Fund Raising Council, New York, 1970.

9. For this insight, I am indebted to Gibson Winter's interesting study, *Religious Identity,* Macmillan, New York, 1968.

10. This eclectic definition is drawn primarily from P. R. Lawrence and J. W. Lorsch's *Developing Organizations,* Addison-Wesley, Reading, Mass. 1969.

11. Mead, Loren B., *The Parish is the Issue,* Project Test Pattern, Washington, revised, November, 1971.

12. *Cf.* mimeographed paper, *Consulting Skills,* Metropolitan Ecumenical Ministry, 969 McCarter Highway, Newark, N.J. 07102.

13. The description is a conflation of material in a mimeographed paper, *Analysis of Council Use of Outside Consultants,* National Council of Churches, New York, May, 1970, and the book, *Process Consultation* by E. H. Schein, Addison-Wesley, Reading, 1969.

14. *Cf.* Schein, *op. cit.*

15. While the literature in this area is not particularly settled, some signs of basic organizational health are
    1. Existence of mutual trust, vertically and laterally.
    2. Collaborative style v. competitive and v. lone wolf.
    3. Decision making located near the relevant information.
    4. Open problem-solving climate not afraid of conflict and change.
    5. Flexibility and use of temporary systems.
    6. Goals of organization clearly owned by all members and members feel responsible for attainment of them.

16. Harbridge House, 11 Arlington St., Boston, Mass. 02116; *Clergy Manpower Management; Deployment and placement,* a pilot study for the Episcopal Diocese of Massachusetts, Sept. 1967, performed in cooperation with the Dioceses of Rhode Island, New Hampshire, Western Massachusetts, and the Committee to Study Clergy and Professional Placement in the Church.

17. For current addresses, contact this author.

18. Write to them at Project Test Pattern, Hearst Hall, Mt. St. Alban, N.W., Washington, D.C. 20016 for the list of copyrighted material now available, and for notice of the books and studies slated for publication in the windup of their communications effort. Of particular interest among things already out are (general) "The Parish is the Issue" and (technical) "Parish Intervention Handbook." Much of my material about them comes from these documents.

19. Hadden, Jeffrey, *The Gathering Storm in the Churches,* Garden City, Doubleday, 1969.

20. Intercultural Studies Group, 8 Newbury St., 4th Fl., Boston, Mass.

CHAPTER EIGHT

Endpiece

Perspective

After a look at some specific institutional difficulties which have made life strange and difficult for people in general in the church, and the clergy in particular, and after a glimpse at some exciting movements which seem to be dealing fruitfully with these problems, perhaps it is wise to step back a pace, and regain our general perspective.

We live in an exciting, threatening period of great and rapid change. It is a "future shock" world. It is a "fail safe" world, in which the possibility of ultimate war looms large.

We are moving from a goods economy, through a period when the economy is dominated by the services sector, into a period when we shall have a knowledge economy.[1] Ninety per cent of the information and knowledge in the whole of recorded history has been generated in our era.

But great issues remain unsolved, and many of them are as old as the beginning of man. There is the issue of war. Will and Ariel Durant, in their summary thoughts after a lifetime of work on a multi-volume history of civilization, recount how few years the world has been without any war raging during its entire recorded life.[2] There is the issue of poverty. For the first time, there is a movement declaring that we are capable of abolishing poverty, that we need not resign ourselves to assuming that "the poor ye have with you always." There is the issue of justice, whether it be raised judicially as the right of every individual to have his day in court, or whether it be raised distributively in the increasing gap between the lot of the world's haves and have-nots. There is the issue of ecology, and how to deal with the pollutions engendered by modern urban-technological society. And finally there is the issue of power, the cry of increasing numbers for a more participative style of decision-making. Ours is a much changed world, yet we are still dealing with some issues of long, long standing.

In this setting, the religious institution, and particularly the Christian church, finds itself in what we have called the "post-Christian state." It came through a "frontier" stage as a minority in an indifferent or even hostile society. It then entered an establishment or "Christendom" stage, in which Christianity was the official religion, and church and state tried to complement each other, even if in rivalry. They saw themselves as two parts of the same integral universe, with the state as the political instrument of the Kingdom of God on earth, and the church as the religious glue of the state. The last two or three generations have seen the emergence of a third stage, the "post-Christian world" in which Christianity is again a minority religion. The religious institution is learning to act again quietly as leaven in society, rather than as a loud and powerful pressure group. Its minority position may cause its luke-warm members to fall away and thus purify the institution, leaving a smaller nucleus of adherents who choose their faith for basic reasons.

In other words, the contemporary church, as at few other times in its existence, has the opportunity to recover and reemphasize its core-functions:[3] 1) telling the good-news story within and without (evangelism and sanctification and nurture); 2) serving (pastoral and community service, social service and social action); 3) living community life (sharing within and without); and 4) worship and prayer (liturgy and meditation within, to rock musicals and celebration without). In the switch from bingo and rummage sales and building maintenance, or from religion as a department of the state, to good-newsing, serving, sharing, and celebrating may come new strengths and meanings for people both within and without the church.

The Twin Movement

A twin movement can be discerned at work during recent years. On the one hand, institutional religion has declined; simultaneously, a movement for Christian renewal is "busting out all over."

The loss of power and centrality in society for the church has meant a loss of status for the clergy. This has a *personal aspect* in that the clergyman must find a new identity, for the old parson image has become one of geniality without specific competence and ceremony without imputed honor. There is also a *work aspect* to the loss, in that the teacher, lawyer, doctor, social worker, and probation worker are doing work which had once been within the pastor's purview.

At the same time, we are witnessing a multiplicity of renewal efforts. The liturgical movement, the revival of religious community life in other communions and the vast changes in monasticism in the Roman Catholic Church, will serve as but a few examples of the rejuvenations that are taking place. It is in the setting of this loss of status and this renewal that the clergy have dealt with three areas of great difficulty in three exciting ways. Or, more properly, the Holy Spirit, in his work of renewal, has enabled a host of good things to happen, and in this book we have singled out three of them which have to do with the brotherhood of the pastorate.

Review

The clergy have been faced with a top-leadership vacuum. There is room at the top because the old autocratic style of leadership is no longer viable. The church, a conservative social institution, is late in abandoning this approach. Consequently, there is a leadership vacuum. It has been our contention that the emergence in our generation of professional clergy associations and academies can do much to fill this vacuum. For the style of leadership in these associations is of peer-group participative decision making. Clergy associations are dealing creatively with lack of peer support by erecting a new kind of professional peer-group structure.

The clergy in many main line denominations have found a situation of too many too-small ministry units, resulting in their not being given sufficient opportunity to function as clergy, but having to do mostly layman's work, and also being given insufficient support for their labors. We have seen solutions in the movement of "tentmaking" clergy, those who combine earning their living in secular jobs with an ecclesiastical ministry for small remuneration.

Finally, many clergy find themselves overeducated and underemployed. This deprives them of the opportunity to function at the professional level. Increasing numbers of clergy have dealt successfully with this situation by being trained and accredited in a variety of specialties and serving as consultants part time. All this represents a creative coping on the part of significant numbers of pastors and parsons in a period of upset and rapid change.

Three Summary Observations

The perspective from which we have approached the ecclesiastical institution in this last third of the twentieth century, and the tour we have taken through the world of peers (clergy associations/academies), tents (non-stipendiary ministries and worker-priesthoods), and owls (clergy serving as outside consultants), has led us to three general observations, all hopeful and action-oriented.

The first is that our time of rapid change is a time of renewal, both potential and actual. Our initial axiom, reiterated in almost every chapter, has been that the time of change we live in can be either threatening or an exciting challenge. There have been many successful experiments in renewal. Some, of course, have failed, possibly for one or more of three reasons. First, there was insufficient administrative undergirding. Second, there was ineffectual communication with the men and women in the pew who were paying the bills. Third, the religious hierarchy, schooled in the "ageless, changeless" approach, were unable to distinguish between renewal-change and change that alters the essence of Christian faith and practice.

The second observation is that this is a time for action. We have a sufficient amount of data, an adequate understanding of problems, and knowledge of tested and fruitful ways toward solutions. We are ready to act and renew. Further study need not be a major item on our agenda.

The American Roman Catholic Church has recently completed, at considerable cost, some helpful studies of theological (Carl Armbruster), psychological (Eugene Kennedy), historical (John Tracy Ellis), and sociological (Andrew Greeley) aspects of the priesthood in the U.S.A. The Episcopal Church has been spending a corresponding sum to support the separate task forces, agencies, commissions, and boards which are trying to coordinate themselves as the Ministry Council. Other religious bodies are in similar situations. But very little has been done officially, even though much has been learned.

This leads to a third observation. The action is to be found on the local or regional scene, in the local congregation and the special ministries, agencies and institutions. The impetus for movement forward is unlikely to come from above. It is coming and must come from the front-line priest, pastor, and administrator. The needful data can be made available to those joining the everincreasing number of renewal groups. And therein is the peer support for a brotherhood that can not only help one another, but also minister to the world and give glory to God Almighty, our Creator and Redeemer and Sanctifier.

Requirements

What is required of us who presently constitute the ordained manpower of the church is a radical reorientation. We were ordained to a ministry we thought possessed a great deal of ascribed status. We find that there is much less than heretofore. We have lost caste; we must learn to make our own way. For some of us, the most honest thing to do will be to make an honorable exit from the pastorate. But for others of us, the reorientation will mean finding again in a new way our vocation to be the servants of the servants of God.

Something different will be required of prospective clergy. Two new facts must be accepted of them at the outset. The first is that one-half of them must be prepared to do their ecclesiastical functioning on top of a secular financial base. Second, they must realize that the ordained ministry is now looked on as a fairly low-status occupation.

From the rest of the church, the whole People of God, we

shall need "straight talk" to the pastors and clergy, combined with responsible participation. Too often we find lay people treating the clergy with kid gloves and exaggerated respect but at the same time not trusting pastors as effective persons and leaving all religious affairs to them. We are looking for Christian persons who complain forthrightly and openly to pastors, and at the same time sweat through problems with them.

And finally something is required of the world in its dealing with the clergy, insofar as it chooses to deal with church at all! It is a facing up to the real issues of life and death, and an openness to people and ideas.

We began this book with a note of excitement and hopefulness. We end with a note of confidence. The church and the clergy of 2000 A.D. will be different in many respects than they were in the 1950's. But the essential things will be the same, and perhaps even more in evidence: the good news to be proclaimed, service to men, a life of love, and celebrating the great joys and tragedies of life and death and rebirth. I have confidence in the renewal of the clergy, based on my experience of recent years. This is because I have confidence in God's Holy Spirit at work in his world.

Footnotes

1. Drucker, Peter F., *The Age of Discontinuity,* New York, Harper & Row, 1968 and 1969.
2. Durant, Will (William James) and Ariel, Supplementary Volume to *The Story of Civilization,* New York, Simon & Schuster, 1935-67.
3. *Cf.* the theses of such men in the field of Church and society as Professor Gabriel Fackre of Androver-Newton Theological School.

DATE DUE

			Printed in USA